SMALL
GAME
HUNTING

AN OUTDOOR LIFE BOOK

SMALL GAME HUNTING

Clyde Ormond

Animal photographs by
Leonard Lee Rue, III

Drawings by
Douglas Allen

OUTDOOR LIFE • FUNK & WAGNALLS
New York

Library of Congress Catalog Card Number: 67–14557
Funk & Wagnalls Hardcover Edition: ISBN 0–308–10328–9
Paperback Edition: ISBN 0–308–10329–7

First Edition, 1967
Two Printings

Second Edition, Revised and Updated, 1977
Fourth Printing, 1979

Manufactured in the United States of America

Contents

To my grandson, Gerald Clyde Ormond, Jr. May he have as happy a time afield after our small game animals as his grandfather has had.

Introduction

The small game of North America offers hunting for anyone to enjoy. Unlike big-game hunting, small-game hunting does not entail extensive planning, extended trips afield, or heavy expense. The hunter need not endure cold, nasty weather as he often must when hunting waterfowl, nor does he have to venture far from home to seek the habitat of a certain upland bird or the tame sport of the paid hunting preserve. Instead, small-game hunting normally requires nothing more elaborate than a walk through the fields or woods near home or a short hike after an equally short drive in the family car.

The happy reason for this is that America is richly endowed with small game animals and birds of varied species and extensive populations widely spread over the entire country. The habitats of these different species often overlap, so that the hunter after one animal may often find another of equal interest to challenge his skill. Added to this is the fact that our smaller game repopulates much faster than do our larger game animals and, with wise game management, provides the country—and hunters—with a continuous supply. Nevertheless, the hunter should always check the game laws of his state to determine whether it is legal to hunt a particular species at any given time. Since game laws change from year to year, this precaution must be taken annually.

Many small game animals are now being hunted on private lands. To earn the privelege of hunting on these lands, the hunter must respect private property, adhere to game laws, and show proper courtesy toward the landowner.

As hunting pressure increases and the populations of small game diminish, hunters will have to be content in the future with smaller game bags and take their rewards from the other benefits of the hunt. Hunters will have to learn, in the interests of their own sport, the value of "leaving some for seed," whether they hunt pests or edible small game.

But small-game hunting is more than just the pursuit of a quarry. Tramping through the autumn woods and breathing the clean air of the outdoors is a reward in itself, and escaping from the necessities of everyday life into the serenity of nature offers the chance for a rebirth of body and spirit. Alone in the woods for hours at a time, the hunter has a chance to observe his surroundings and gain an insight into the creative balance which keeps our physical world in equilibrium. Best of all, small-game hunting is a fine way to introduce a young person to the beauties of field and wood, to instill in him a love of the outdoors and a respect for firearms, and to teach him the virtues of self-reliance and responsibility.

CLYDE ORMOND
Rigby, Idaho

CHUCKS

Woodchuck

1

Woodchuck

A FEW GENERATIONS or so ago, when firearms and cartridges were developed to the point where a 50-grain bullet could be driven at velocities of 3,000 foot-seconds and over, the lowly woodchuck became a highly prized species to the fraternity of skilled riflemen. The woodchuck changed overnight from a crop-destroying rodent into a badge of honor to the shooter who could take him consistently at 200, 300, and 400 yards.

The eastern woodchuck *(Marmota monax)* is a squat, ground-hugging animal of brown-rust coloration. Adults will reach 24 inches in overall length and weigh up to 10 pounds and over. The woodchuck has a flattish, hairy tail around 6 inches long, a keen nose, exceptionally sensitive eyes, and a pair of puny but exceptionally keen ears. In its general appearance the woodchuck suggests an enlarged version of a western ground squirrel.

The woodchuck is a vegetarian and loves grain, alfalfa, and other domestic crops, as well as the natural grasses which grow in his habitat. The range of this brown rodent includes all the eastern part of the United States from Oklahoma towards the Atlantic. This overall range extends up into British Columbia and even Alaska. The largest woodchuck population, however, is in the northeastern states.

This species is open to hunting only from spring until he goes into hibernation in early fall. Usually this occurs before the first fall frosts, depending on the region. The animal emerges at about the beginning of the spring softening and melting of snow.

Birth of the young, usually in litters of from four to a half-dozen, takes place during hibernation. The young will come from the dens soon after they are born in late April and May and play about nearby.

The enemies of the woodchuck are coyotes, bears, wolves, foxes, eagles, and man. The singular protection against these enemies is the chuck's burrow or den. At the first sign of danger—and this includes the sight of man at great distances—the chuck will run down his burrow. He usually won't emerge until all danger, as interpreted by his sensitive special senses, is gone. Seldom does a chuck venture great distances from his burrow. He can't outrun his enemies, so he simply makes his part of the race shorter.

Because of his timid nature and keen alertness to any danger, hunting this species is something of an art, requiring high shooting skill, precision equipment, and great patience.

The first step is to locate chucks by investigating the terrain and studying any available spoor. Within their general habitat, chucks favor places where they can dig —semibrushy dikes and fencerows, meadows, sidehills and small knolls. These are the animal's home, maternity ward, and sanctum. In the short treks from their domiciles, chucks leave narrow trails through foliage; tracks resembling a muskrat's only larger; and green dung curved in shape and ⅜ inch in diameter. Often while scouting for these signs the hunter will spot an animal feeding in a meadow or standing upright by his burrow.

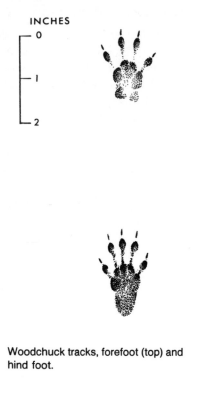

INCHES

0

1

2

Woodchuck tracks, forefoot (top) and hind foot.

Pattern of woodchuck tracks.

Rifle for long-range chuck shooting should be sighted in properly before the hunt. Homemade bench like this one holds rifle steady.

A simpler way, if you are a beginner, is to ask a landowner on whose property you wish to hunt if he has any chucks. If the landowner gives you permission to hunt, he'll usually tell you where to find the chucks.

Once you find the animals or their sign, the best hunting procedure is to post yourself at considerable distance from any fresh chuck workings and wait patiently. Good places to wait are edges of woodland at the border of open grassy meadows, behind knolls, fencerows, and similar cover. In waiting out a chuck, you should remain low—a standing hunter, ablaze in gaudy-colored clothing, is a sign of danger to any species. Once the chuck shows outside his burrow, it's up to you to make your one shot count. A missed chuck will disappear, maybe for hours, and becomes wary and gunshy.

The best woodchuck rifles are the most accurate, flat-shooting weapons available. More weight may be tolerated in these rifles than in big-game rifles, since they

Bipod of two sticks tied with a handkerchief forms a rest for long-range shooting. Sitting position is steady, gives a clear view of the terrain.

normally aren't carried as far each day. Scope sights are the only kind a veteran chuck hunter will use, since they allow more precise placement of the bullet.

Bolt-action rifles are the best for hunting woodchucks. This system of breeching is generally necessary to handle the high-intensity cartridges currently used. The Winchester Model 70, Remington Model 700, Savage Model 112-V, Weatherby, and many commercial and custom rifles using the Mauser FN Model 400 Series action are all fine choices. The recent Ruger custom single-shot rifle, in proper caliber, should make an ideal arm for the purpose. Any chuck rifle should have the inherent capacity to send the bullet from a suitable cartridge at minute-of-angle precision, or roughly an inch per 100 yards. This accuracy should extend to a range of 400 yards, all shots remaining in a 4-inch circle at this range.

Ormond Swing is easily made of 40-inch length of No. 10 galvanized wire and buckskin shoelace. Ends of the wire are pushed into the ground; the rifle is rested on the lace.

The rifle is only an instrument sending its missile at a certain velocity, at a given twist, and with a certain degree of accuracy. The cartridge for woodchuck hunting is of equal if not greater importance.

Briefly, a chuck cartridge should send a bullet of 50 to 100 grains (depending upon caliber and cartridge) at velocities of 3,000 foot-seconds and upward, with target accuracy. Following are some of the best woodchuck cartridges:

Cartridge	Bullet Weight	Velocity
.222 Remington	50	3200
.222 Remington Magnum	55	3300
.22/250 Remington	55	3800
.223 Remington	55	3300
.224 Weatherby Varmintmaster	50	3700
.225 Winchester	55	3600
.243 Winchester	80	3500
6 mm. Remington	80	3500

Of these, the fine little .222 Remington will take care of a majority of the shots at woodchucks, assuming that the hunter is a careful stalker, wears camouflage clothing, and remains concealed. The .222 is a cartridge adequate on chucks to 225 yards. For shots out to 300 yards, the .22/250, .223, .224, and .225 calibers are better. And for those extreme shots at around 400 yards, and where wind is a factor, the 6 mm. and .243 will make hits where the .22 calibers will fall off. With these two, the hunter pays in more report and an increased but acceptable amount of recoil.

To bring out the accuracy of such cartridges and rifles, a scope of high power is vital. For chuck hunting, the power of the scope should be at least 8X, or 8 magnification. Eight to 10 power is ideal for chucks out to 400 yards, though many use higher power target-type scopes. Many of today's variable scopes will reach this magnification, and the Weaver, Bushnell, Leupold, and Redfield variables all make good woodchuck scopes. A fine one is Redfield's recent 12X. So is Weaver's V9. A medium-fine crosshair is the best reticle for chucks.

Ormond Swing in use. Note that left hand does not support fore-end but presses the buttplate firmly against right shoulder.

Hits on chucks at 200 yards and over can only be made if the rifle is held firmly in the prone or sitting position, or some variation of these positions. Some hunters use a bipod under the rifle's fore-end to steady it.

A bipod can be quickly made in the field by tying a handkerchief around the intersection of two sticks, so that two opposing V's are created. Two legs of the bipod are put on the ground, and the rifle rested on the top V.

The best bipod I've ever used is of my own design. I call it the Ormond Swing and it's been patented. To make it, bend a 40-inch length of No. 10 galvanized wire at the center until it becomes an inverted U, with legs 6 inches apart. At the top, or center, wrap a buckskin shoelace spirally down each leg for about 6 inches, ending each wrapping with two half-hitches. Tie the two ends of lace together, forming a tight, shallow V. The rifle's fore-end is rested on this "swing." The height may be regulated by the amount the legs are pushed into the ground. The rifle is held as in prone position with the difference that the left hand (for right-handed shooters) doesn't hold the fore-end, but presses the buttplate tightly against the right shoulder. This provides a firmly anchored "tripod," with enough give to the spring so that the rifle won't "shoot away," as it would if rested solidly on top of a log or other hard surface. When not in use, this light little swing is handily carried by looping it to the rear of your belt.

Western Rockchuck

2

Rockchuck

THE WESTERN counterpart of the eastern woodchuck is the rockchuck *(Marmota caligata)*. For practical hunting purposes the two are comparable. Each is of similar size, has many of the same habits, and like many species of wildlife, varies in coloration according to his habitat.

The interest in rockchuck hunting in the West is a recent development. For decades riflemen ignored the brown rodent because of the abundance of big game. The rockchuck was considered "kids' stuff." But with the increase in hunting pressure, serious riflemen have turned to this animal as a real challenge to their hunting and shooting skills.

Rockchucks inhabit a wide area of country westward from the Great Plains, and from the southern part of Alberta, Canada, to the Mexican border. A great share of the population is concentrated in the Rocky Mountain region. The basic difference between the woodchuck and the rockchuck is that the former loves the fields, woodlands, and rich farmlands of the East, whereas his cousin likes the rocky regions of the West.

Overlapping the range of the rockchuck is another species of marmot, the yellow-footed marmot *(Marmota flaviventris)*. This species is distributed through the Black Hills of South Dakota and the Bear Lodge Mountains of Wyoming, as well as over western Canada and Alaska. In the Far North he is referred to simply as the "whistling marmot," or "whistler"—a name given him by the French.

The rockchuck inhabits the desert sagebrush lands, the rocky slides, outcroppings, and rims of lava-rock gorges and canyons, and bluffs and buttes of broken rocks rising from desert flats. The animals hibernate in dens in these protected places and upon emergence find their food at the peripheries, where grasses and foliage grow in more fertile earth. Where such regions occur at the edges of marginal farmlands which produce grain and alfalfa, the rockchuck is in his glory. He can take short treks from his den, feed, and retreat to the protection of rocks.

Hibernation usually occurs by early August, later in the warmer regions. Emergence is dependent on the coming of spring, but is generally in late March or April. Occasionally a chuck will show up when snow is still on the ground.

The big difference between hunting the woodchuck and the rockchuck lies in the angle of the country, which necessitates a different stalking and shooting technique. Where the eastern variety is normally found in easy rolling country, the western chuck loves those rocky bluffs, gorge sides, and lava outcroppings which would embarrass a mountain goat. The farther these places are from farmlands and contact with man, the better, since the rockchuck is a timid soul. To locate, stalk, and shoot chucks in such places, requires special know-how.

One favored method in the West is to hunt the desert sagebrush and lava outcrop areas with a jeep-type vehicle. Only such an outfit will negotiate this kind of terrain without wrecking, since there are usually no roads and the ground is full of holes and hub-high boulders. There are still numerous such desert regions in the West.

Usually two or more hunters will go as a party—one drives, the others watch the

INCHES

Rockchuck tracks, forefoot (top) and hind foot.

Pattern of rockchuck tracks, walking.

Spotting scope set up on the hood of vehicle is an aid in finding rockchucks on distant ridges.

bluffs and high, rocky rims. The chucks are either spotted as they lie and sun themselves like flat furry bricks atop the rocks, or as they move in and out from den areas to feeding grounds in the flatter lands below.

Good accessories for locating rockchucks are spotting scopes, binoculars, and the high-powered scope on the sniping rifle. One good way is to stop parallel to a distant ridge or rimrock, then set up a spotting scope on your vehicle's hood.

Once you locate some chucks, stalk them on foot, keeping the general unevenness of the terrain between yourself and the quarry. Sometimes you can drive to within shooting distance. When you are within range—anywhere from 175 to 400 yards—assume a solid shooting position. Often you can use the top of the vehicle hood, which offers nearly a benchrest position if a coat is laid over it. The legality of this should be carefully checked first. Many states prohibit shooting game from a vehicle. Some allow shooting at varmints only, except from a road. Unlike in woodchuck shooting, it is rarely possible to take an orthodox prone position when hunting

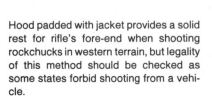

Hood padded with jacket provides a solid rest for rifle's fore-end when shooting rockchucks in western terrain, but legality of this method should be checked as some states forbid shooting from a vehicle.

11

Good strategy is to post yourself on a rocky rim and wait for rockchucks to come out of their burrows. Shoot from a solid position.

rockchucks. Because of the terrain, awkward stances are often required.

Another method of rockchuck hunting is to find a rocky gorge where chucks are working, post yourself at the opposing rim and wait patiently for the appearance of a brown form. Shoot from the most solid position possible.

An experienced hunter who is a capable whistler can often induce a chuck to show himself at a distance. The right sound is a short, sharp, high-pitched *wheet*. This simulates the natural chirp of an old chuck and will often bring one out to investigate. The lower the hunter stays to the ground, the more apt the chuck is to show, and the higher he is apt to perch.

12

A third method is simply to walk them up. In an area known to contain chucks, simply move along the rocky terrain, studying all likely spots. The chuck will generally show up as a running form, a dark vertical object which doesn't quite blend with the landscape, or a flattened brown form on the top of a rock.

In western rockchuck hunting, once in a great while you will find pure black rockchucks. Melanism is rare in rockchucks but does exist. I have seen and killed black rockchucks in the Snake River-Teton area of eastern Idaho, and a few years ago Glidden McNeel, the Wyoming outfitter, and I saw three pure black chucks along a rocky wall near Mosquito Creek in Wyoming. It was late September during an elk hunt, and all chucks normally should have been hibernating in that area by then. Possibly it was a forecast of our mild late fall.

The same rifles and cartridges used for woodchucks are ideal for rockchucks. Many of the older cartridges, such as the older .220 Swift, .250 Savage, .257 Roberts, .22 Hornet, and .22 Neidner Magnum, are still used for western chucks. This is partly because many hunters have them, or have used the larger calibers to double on deer and antelope later in the season. For the same reason, others use the .270 and .30/06 with lighter bullets speeded up for varmints.

The more dedicated of the clan are going largely to such calibers as the .222 Remington, .223 Remington, .225 Winchester, .22/250 (the old Varminter now commercialized), and the .243. A few have tried the .264 Magnum, with 100-grain bullets, for long-range shots or for days when a wind would blow post holes out of the ground. Actually, the .222 Remington will take care of a majority of shots at rockchucks. But if one caliber had to be used on this species by veteran chuckers, it would be the .22/250. This caliber approaches the ideal rockchuck cartridge. The recent .17 Remington cartridge has gained some attention as a rockchuck cartridge, but its light bullet won't buck wind well at longer ranges.

The .243 is gaining in popularity, especially by those who hunt on windy days and who must use the same rifle for deer and antelope. The .264 is seldom needed for rockchucks. It has too much recoil, too much blast, and no real advantage over the range of a .243 since the shooter can't hold on chucks much farther than a .243 will explode them.

Like eastern woodchuck hunters, chuck hunters in the West aren't long at the game until they are confirmed reloaders. My own pet loads for the .222, .243, and .22/250 are:

.222 Remington with 21 grains of #4198 powder and 50-grain Hornady or Speer bullets.

.243 Winchester using 36 grains of #4895 powder, Winchester #120 primers, and 70-grain Hornady spire-point bullets.

.22/250, with 35 grains #4895 powder, 50-grain Speer or Hornady bullets.

The whistling marmot of the Far North isn't hunted much, except in conjunction with big-game hunting. Occasionally a hunter will bang away at one, but he hates to frighten big game in the area with so much noise. My own first whistler is a good example. In British Columbia, while hunting grizzlies, I shot a whistler at 150 yards.

As the pieces floated down, I had the firm conviction that a .300 H&H was too much for chucks and that there wouldn't be enough left to photograph. The whistler there has the dubious distinction of being the last food the grizzlies eat before going into hibernation, and I left this one already chewed for them.

RABBITS and
HARES

Cottontail Rabbit

3

Cottontail

THE COTTONTAIL rabbit is our most hunted animal, for two reasons. First, the cottontail is the most widely distributed game species in America. The small, gray *Sylvilagus* ranges throughout most of North America. Secondly, with a gestation period of slightly less than a month, this timid little bunny seems bent not only on keeping hunters supplied with quarry but on supporting such predators as foxes, eagles, coyotes, owls, hawks, and rats.

This ubiquitous species is small as game goes. An adult will weigh 2 to 3 pounds and reach an overall length of slightly over 1 foot. Both sexes are gray in coloration, and the pelage doesn't change in color with the coming of winter. Litters average about four.

Almost any kind of habitat will suffice for the cottontail, which was named for his white tail. He likes brushy dikes, weed patches, fencerows, ditches, and similar thick cover into which he can escape from enemies. Cottontails will go down burrows, especially in desert or lava country where foliage is sparse. When danger is apparent, the cottontail breaks into a short burst of speed, his white tail bobbing up and down like a jumping snowball. Like other species, a cottontail will leave an avenue of escape open. At the end of his short run, he will usually pause unless hard-pressed, then either sit still to ascertain the extent of the danger, or run down a hole in the rocks, into the protection of a brush pile or a burrow left by some larger animal.

As with some species of grouse, the population cycle has its peak and its low point. Peak populations occur about every decade, as do the years of extreme cottontail scarcity. Each year rain, disease, predators, and the first heavy frosts of fall cut into the cottontail supply. By late hunting season, only a fraction of the crop has survived. Then the species must start its program of replenishment all over again. Low ebb is from September until April. In the warmer climates of the South, cottontails breed all year long. In northern climates, they reproduce only during summer months.

The ubiquitousness of the cottontail plus his pattern of escape dictate when and how he is hunted.

The bird hunter, tramping between conveys, often flushes a cottontail from the weed cover of bird habitat and shoots him with a shotgun as he bobs away. Or the big-game hunter, after rolling his buck, will see a cottontail at a rock patch and make a head shot for some pot-meat. Again, the boy hunter, tramping the fields with his .22 and actually bent on a crow if he can get close enough, will see a cottontail rabbit sunning himself outside a badger hole and decide on the whiter meat.

Every type of firearm has been used on cottontails. When using a high-calibered arm, the hunter always tries to make a head shot, since the meat of the species is very palatable—partly why he is hunted. There is only one consistently successful way to shoot running cottontails, however, and that's with a shotgun.

The shotgun used on upland birds or waterfowl is suitable for cottontails, and one of the best is a 12 gauge with modified or other reasonably open choke. A wide pattern spread is desirable. Number 6 and 7½ shot are fine, and the low-powered shells are sufficient as most cottontails are shot at close ranges. The 20 gauge, too, is a fine cottontail gun.

The type of gun isn't so vital as in waterfowl or upland bird shooting, since one shot is average for cottontails: at the bang of the gun the rabbit is either pot-meat or gone into a hole or brush. Perhaps a single-barreled shotgun in the hands of an enthusiastic youngster will kill more cottontails than many another combination.

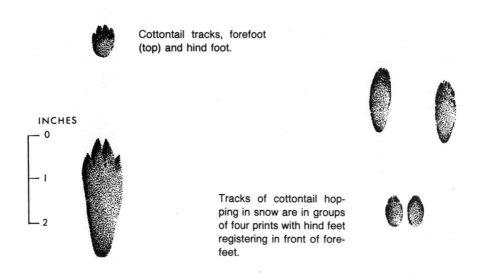

Cottontail tracks, forefoot (top) and hind foot.

INCHES

0

1

2

Tracks of cottontail hopping in snow are in groups of four prints with hind feet registering in front of forefeet.

Shotgun is best weapon for hunting cottontails. Gunner must have quick reflexes to hit a running rabbit before it disappears into a burrow or brushpile.

Dogs are very useful in cottontail hunting. The dog hunts by scent, finds the quarry, and flushes it before the hunter. Which way the bunny will go is always interesting, but the hunter is assured of a fast race and a quick shot, with Rover trying his best to catch up.

One of the best cottontail dogs is the Beagle. This merry little fellow loves to hunt rabbits, is a pleasant companion for any small-game hunter, and generally flushes the rabbits close enough before the hunter so there is opportunity for a shot. Larger dogs often run the game clear out of the area before a shouting and laboring hunter can catch up. Two hunters working cottontail cover with a slow-working dog often have a real advantage. If the game bounds one way, one hunter has his chance—and vice versa.

Because the species will sit unless pressed, and because it is possible to approach him at relatively close range, hunting cottontails with bow and arrow and handgun has become increasingly popular. Archers generally use blunt arrows rather than broadheads. Handgunners often use the .22 rimfire, .22 WMR, .38 Special, and even the magnum calibers. With the .38 Special and larger calibers, mid-range loads are normally used, with wad-cutter type bullets. This combination kills quickly, without undue damage to the meat. Skilled handgun shooters, however, try whenever possible to make head shots, to save the delicious meat. An archer or a handgun hunter would rather make one kill on cottontails with his pet weapon in a day's hunting than to take a dozen rabbits with a shotgun or rifle.

Here, by the way, is the recipe for a fine stew to make of that cottontail:

1	cottontail
2	quarts boiling water
1	cup corn
1	cup lima beans
1	onion
1	cup tomatoes
2	small potatoes
1½	teaspoons salt
½	teaspoon pepper (black)
1½	teaspoon sugar
¼	cup butter

Dress the rabbit by removing insides through a cut made from pelvis to neck along the abdomen, and by splitting both pelvis and ribcage. Skin the carcass, wash clean of all blood and body juices, and cut into six to eight pieces.

To the boiling water, add the rabbit, corn, lima beans, potatoes, onion, salt, and pepper. Cover pot and simmer (do not boil) for two hours. Add tomatoes and sugar, and simmer for another hour. Lastly, add butter and simmer for ten minutes. Bring to a full boil and serve.

This will serve three to four average hunters—if hungry hunters can ever be said to be average.

4

Snowshoe Rabbit

A BASIC difference between a hare and a rabbit is that the young of the hare are born furred and with eyes open. Those of the rabbit are born naked and with eyes closed.

The snowshoe rabbit *(Lepus americanus)* is really a hare. He is nearly as well known by the name varying hare. This name is appropriate because the pelage of this species changes during the winter from gray-brown summer coat to pure white, with the exception of ear tips and eyes. This coloration change gives the hare protection against enemies such as wolves, coyotes, owls, and eagles. In summer the drab color blends with the foliage of the bush and forest country, and in winter the white matches the snow.

I have found three game species in white winter garb very hard to see even at close range. These are the ptarmigan, snowshoe rabbit, and the ermine or weasel. If the animal is not in motion, the first thing one detects is the jet-black eyes. These seem incongruous in a dazzling white setting, but with closer scrutiny the contour of the entire creature becomes plain.

The snowshoe rabbit is larger than the cottontail but smaller than the jack rabbit. Adults average about 2½ to 3½ pounds. Besides the changing coat, this hare is identified by his enormous hind feet, from which he gets his name. These are all out of proportion to his forefeet, and are an example of nature's provision for the survival of a species. The large hind feet ride upon loose snow literally like snowshoes, allowing the rabbit to outrun heavier enemies like the bobcat and coyote. They flounder; he runs.

Snowshoe Rabbit in Winter Coat

Snowshoe Rabbit in Summer Coat

Like the cottontail, the varying hare is cyclic, the crests and depressions of this cycle occurring every seven to ten years. During an abundant year, the female snowshoe rabbit will bear up to eight in a litter. There is a fundamental connection between a scarce year and the litter number. During a low year, the annual litter of the snowshoe bunny may drop to around two per female.

The range of the varying hare covers most of the wooded portions of northern America, especially the conifer areas. The range extends into southeastern Alaska and covers most of Canada. During the summer the snowshoe rabbit eats clover, dandelions, and such green plants as are found in forested regions. In winter he changes his diet to bark and willow twigs.

The varying hare is timid like all rabbits but depends more on speed in getting away from enemies than does the cottontail. When you come upon a hare of this species, he will generally hop away but stop at what he considers a safe distance. If pursued, the animal will then make another short hopping run, and pause again. This hare won't depend on going into a burrow after its run, as does the cottontail, but makes this continuing series of escape-runs.

I had occasion to observe this once in the Yukon. Guide Herb Leake and I were after grizzlies, but the route took us through a whole mountainside of short scrub willows and Arctic birch. On that one mountainside, we counted just over 100 snowshoe rabbits, sometimes three to six flushing away from the saddle horses at once. These always seem to stop, mostly in a semi-open area, at about 100 yards from us. This distance from danger was apparently their safety quotient.

Tracks of snowshoe rabbit showing large hind foot, small forefoot.

INCHES

0

1

2

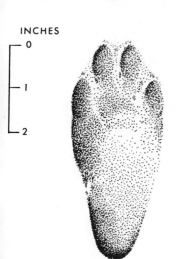

Tracks of snowshoe bounding in snow; hind feet register in front of forefeet.

Don DeHart, Alaska outfitter, demonstrates the best position for shooting snowshoe rabbits with a handgun: two-hand grip with elbows on knees.

Two methods of hunting are suggested by this behavior. First, the hunter on foot can flush the rabbits and take them with a shotgun as they run away. A good gun is the standard 12 gauge, often used for ptarmigan and other upland birds. A modified choke is perhaps best, and a repeater is often needed, either for a second shot at a missed rabbit or when two jump out at once. For the capable shotgun man, a 20 gauge, especially in modern high-power loadings, is entirely adequate. Number 6 and 7½ shot are ideal. The second type of shooting is done with a .22 rimfire rifle shooting hollow-point ammunition. Incidentally, no .22 rimfire bullets of solid construction should ever be used on any type of small game—it doesn't kill well but just drills through. In .22 rimfire shooting, the rifle should be a repeater for obvious reasons. It is best when scope-equipped with sights of low magnification—2 to 3X —and low-mounted. The Weaver C series, Bushnell Banner, and Redfield Sportster are examples of good, inexpensive scopes for the purpose. Most of them have bases which fit into the integral grooved receivers of such modern .22's as the Winchester 270 series and Remington's Models 552 and 572 repeaters.

A vital factor in such shooting (besides plenty of ammunition) is an odd combination of shooting stance and trigger-pull. Much of the shooting will be offhand, due both to a normal short pause, or "set," on the part of the quarry and the usual intervening foliage and brush. This calls for quick shooting, not snap shooting. The standard squeeze-till-it-goes-off recommended for most rifle shooting doesn't apply. Instead, you must get off the shot when the first sight-picture is right. Apply pressure quickly on the trigger, not with an inward squeeze of the whole hand, but largely with the trigger-finger alone. The pull should be reasonably light and crisp. The trigger must actually be pulled by the lone finger without upsetting the inertia of the rifle. A sloppy or delayed trigger-pull won't do the job.

These two methods of hunting will take care of most snowshoe rabbits. In Alaska, while going to or from big-game country during the rabbit season, I have often heard the loud banging of shotguns interspersed by the mild pip-pip of .22's. The local hunters, utilizing the trails and horse routes through the heavy bush for easier going, were walking the country and either shooting snowshoes with shotguns as they broke from cover at close range or taking them farther away on the "set" with .22 rimfires. Often a party of two hunters was equipped with a shotgun and a .22 rifle.

Snowshoe rabbits often are hunted with dogs. A dog adds a new dimension to the sport. A rabbit flushed from cover at close range has great enthusiasm for leaving an area and won't stop as long as dogs are in pursuit. Often he'll run a full mile, in a general circle. This calls for a shotgun, and it is comparable to shooting cottontails flushed before a dog.

In the northern states, snowshoe rabbits often are hunted in the snow. A bounding white target in a field of white snow is deceptive and calls for fast gun work and good eyesight. One of the best arms for this type of shooting is a pump shotgun in modified choke using low-powered shells.

Archers and handgun hunters, hunting without dogs, can get close enough to the varying hare to make their short-range weapons effective—roughly, within 40 yards. Such hunting depends on patience and stalking skill. The use of camouflage clothing —mottled in autumn and white in winter—greatly helps in this. Also, it helps if the hunter can get into areas where the game hasn't been overly hunted.

Once in The Selway Forest, trying for a close-up picture of a varying hare, I got to within 8 feet of him. The rabbit sat and watched me as I approached inch by inch from 50 yards away. As this was primitive area, the bunny probably had never seen a human being. This kind of careful stalking is necessary for the archer or handgun hunter.

Jack Rabbit

5

Jack Rabbit

THE JACK rabbit is one of our true desert dwellers. His gray coloration and his ability to leap nearly as high as an average man and twice that distance along the ground have combined to insure his survival in a region of little water, gray sagebrush, and fleet enemies. In addition, his capacity for rapid reproduction in great numbers assures a continuation of the species.

Like the snowshoe, the jack rabbit is a true hare. The two best-known species are the white-tailed jack rabbit *(Lepus townsendii)* and the black-tailed jack rabbit *(Lepus californicus)*. They range throughout the plains regions of the West from Canada to Mexico. Except for a subspecies which lives in the low mountains, their overall habitat consists of those remaining desert areas of low elevation with sagebrush and similar foliage. When marginal farmlands in these desert areas are irrigated, the jack rabbits remain at the outskirts. Diet consists of most green plants, including prickly pear and domestic alfalfa, the latter being the favorite food when available.

The jack rabbit is built like a greyhound—for running. His legs are long in proportion to his body, though his frame is thin and lanky. His ears are proportionately much longer than those of the cottontail or varying hare. Adults weigh up to 5 pounds and grow to 20 inches in length.

Enemies of the jack rabbit are foxes, coyotes, eagles, bobcats, and man. To escape from danger, the animal relies on his running in a zig-zag pattern of high jumps and long leaps. This species won't ordinarily go down holes but will outrun most enemies. The average dog can't outrun a jack rabbit, but greyhounds and other breeds developed especially for wolf and coyote coursing can. Three coyotes can wear down a jack rabbit by running it in relays before closing in for the kill.

As with other hares and rabbits, there are peak years, years of average populations, and years of rabbit famine.

In the early settlement of the West, the jack rabbit was both a food for the settlers and a great agricultural pest. I have an elderly neighbor whose family homesteaded about a mile from the homestead of my own Dad. This fellow swears that, as kids, his family "ate so many jack rabbits that every time we'd hear a dog bark, we'd lay back our ears and run down a hole under the log house." Actually, the meat of a healthy young jack rabbit is fine food. But at that time, the adult rabbits developed large blisters under their hide, and the pioneers had to give up eating them.

The jack rabbits then were great agricultural pests. As the sagebrush was railed off (two span of horses were hitched to either end of a railroad rail and pulled it over the sage to break it off), and crops and gardens and orchards planted, the jacks turned from sagebrush and prickly pear to domestic foods. They girdled the bark from young fruit trees; ate at stacked alfalfa (mostly at night when they couldn't be scared off) until the stacks tipped over; and nibbled at the settlers' gardens until the rows were bare.

As a boy I have seen many an orchard whose tree trunks were painted with white lead to discourage jack rabbits; many a tipped-over haystack; and many a rabbit drive, when hundreds of the desert rabbits were driven with long rows of net-wire fencing into a large pen and slaughtered.

As late as 1940, commercial processing plants were set up in the Mud Lake— Roberts section of eastern Idaho, and during the winter hunters shot and brought in jack rabbits by the thousands. The animals were skinned for hat makers, and the flesh was processed into mink food for fur ranches. Many a hunter, during those

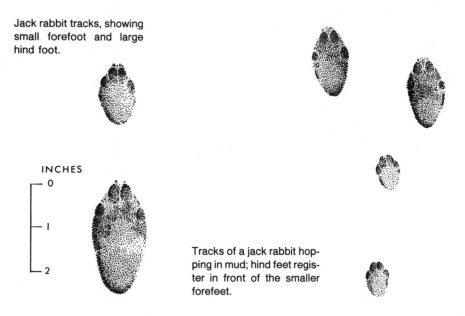

Jack rabbit tracks, showing small forefoot and large hind foot.

INCHES

0

1

2

Tracks of a jack rabbit hopping in mud; hind feet register in front of the smaller forefeet.

years, shot 100 jack rabbits a day, sold the animals for 14 cents each to a processor, and went back hunting the next day.

That day is long gone. The jack rabbit's numbers have diminished, and the species is now looked on by hunters as purely a sporting proposition, Jacks are no longer shot as pure pests except by ranchers and farmers. Hunters are even learning to keep some for seed, to provide ample numbers for the future.

If you want to hunt jack rabbits, you must first find regions where they are relatively abundant and it is legal to hunt. This information should be obtained from the fish and game department. Ranchers in desert regions are usually glad to grant permission to hunt marginal farmlands, once assured that the hunter is responsible and won't shoot at stock or leave gates open.

The most common method of hunting jack rabbits is to hike across desert country until you see a jack rabbit, shoot it on the run, or wait until he "sets" for a long shot off-hand.

Another method is to hunt with a dog and shoot the rabbit as he is flushed from cover. This can provide tricky shooting as the animal darts in and out of high sagebrush.

A better way, requiring more precise aiming, is to hunt with a .22 rimfire repeating rifle—a single-shot is a terrible aggravation. Such a rifle should be scope-equipped, sighted in for 100 yards, and used only with long-rifle hollow-points.

The best two positions for such shooting are little known but effective. One is an offhand stance with the nongrip hand back near the receiver, elbow on uplifted hip, body reared back. This is steadier than the conventional offhand position. A better one is to squat as though sitting on the heels, holding the elbows on the knees. Both positions permit shooting over low, intervening sagebrush.

A sporting form of jack-rabbit hunting is to shoot at them, either on the run or "set," with a varmint rifle. Often jacks won't stop within .22 rimfire range—out to 125 yards—but will pause at 175 to 200 yards. This makes for ideal pest shooting. A good cartridge out at 125 yards is the .22 WMR. It is much more effective than the .22 rimfire but costs more to shoot. Better cartridges for the longer ranges are the .222 Remington, .22 Hornet, .223 Remington, .224 Weatherby, .225 Winchester; and up to the dual-purpose cartridges like the .243 Winchester, 6 mm. Remington, and .257 Roberts. Shooting at running jacks with these last cartridges is great sport and good practice for big game.

In any type of hunting, the shooter should habitually make sure he shoots into the *ground* at some visible distance—not where there's a possibility of a bullet richocheting into a farm or settlement.

Tularemia poses some threat with most species of rabbits, and gloves should be worn when handling dead bunnies.

If you'd like to try eating a healthy young jack rabbit, here's how to skin him in thirty seconds flat:

Twist the skin above both hocks until it breaks. Run a forefinger under the skin between leg and tail on each side at the back, and break it. Pull the skin loose gently around tail, anus, and genitals. Then, holding the animal by the heels with one hand, pull the "cased" skin downward over the entire body. Where the half-skinned elbows of the front legs become exposed, stick a finger through between skin and meat and pull. The skin will break off all around the forelegs at the wrists. Do the same at the ears—get a finger between ears and skin, pull, and peel. Break the skin off at the nose by more pulling. The skinned rabbit will have only small patches of fur left at the nose, genitals, and "mittens." It all takes quite a little less time than it has taken me to write this.

6

Arctic Hare

THE ARCTIC hare *(Lepus articus)* is the largest hare in North America. This hare will reach 2 feet in overall length, and adult males will weigh 12 pounds and over.

Like other species which inhabit cold climates, the Arctic hare mates and reproduces only during the early summer, in April and May. The nest, which serves as a place of concealment, is partially lined with hair the female pulls from her chest. A half-dozen leverets is an average litter. During mating season, these hares are somewhat gregarious and band together, the sexes mingling until the mating season is over, when they go their solitary ways.

The Arctic hare changes its pelage with the season. During summer months, he is predominantly gray with lighter underbelly. With late fall and coming snow, this coloration changes to a pure white, save for the ear tips. While resting, these ears twitch back and forth, probably as the animal listens for enemies, which include weasels, larger owls, Canadian lynx, and foxes.

The general habitat of the Arctic hare is northward of the conifer belt in North America. However, this hare or a subspecies gets much farther south in limited numbers. I have been observing them, and hunting them occasionally, for forty years in the Upper Snake River Valley of Idaho. In this region, the hares prefer the open stubble fields and fallow ground at the periphery of aspen groves. In the fall I have often flushed one of them from a low furrow in the plowed ground. The hare depends on his concealment for protection until you come within 5 to 10 yards. Then he springs forth and bounds away.

This bounding, galloping gait is most interesting to watch. It is not the easy-flowing rhythm of other bounding rabbits or hares. This hare leaves the ground in a long, loping bound, with the animal possibly a foot and a half off the ground, its body entirely "frozen" except for its forward motion. Then, as it comes to the earth, the feet hit the ground daintily, and the hare sails for another 8 to 12 feet. The oddest part of this gait is that the hare's powerful hind feet do not follow the precise course of his front feet but are obliquely off to one side.

In winter this hare still prefers the open fields. He will rest in depressions in the snow, just as he uses forms in the dirt during autumn. Unlike the varying hare, he does not depend on tree cover but counts on his great speed and capacity to run long distances to outdistance his enemies.

Hunting this great hare is obviously something of a specialized technique. Normally, when flushed, he races away in great bounds to distances from 100 to 200 yards. Then, if not hotly pursued, he stops at 100 to 200 yards away and watches his backtrack. You can shoot him as he romps away or, preferably, when he stops. A good cartridge for this is the .22 WMR in a repeating rifle. If you prefer running shots, this will give you ample opportunity to score. If you wait for a standing shot, the cartridge is adequate out to 150 yards or so, which will normally cover the distance to that first important stop.

A better outfit for the occasional long-range standing shot is the accurate little .222 Remington cartridge in a bolt-action rifle equipped with a 4- to 6-power scope. The sitting position provides the best stability.

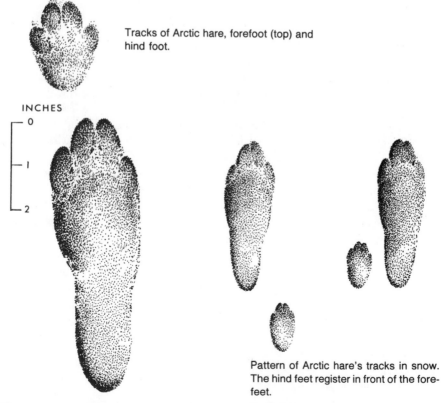

Tracks of Arctic hare, forefoot (top) and hind foot.

INCHES

0

1

2

Pattern of Arctic hare's tracks in snow. The hind feet register in front of the fore-feet.

SQUIRRELS

Gray Squirrel

Fox Squirrel

Red Squirrel

7

Tree Squirrels

SQUIRREL HUNTING is different from the noisy, gregarious sport of coon hunting. For this kind of slow, contemplative sport, the hunter must possess great patience and the ability to remain still for long periods of time. It is said that a successful squirrel hunter can sit so long and so motionless against a hickory tree that his beard will grow through the bole, and the only sound he will make is that of growing old.

Squirrels, like raccoons, were harvested by the Indians before the settlement of America. In the early days of the white man, the supply of squirrels, like that of wild pigeons and buffalo, was thought to be without end. But as the forests were cut down, the squirrel supply dwindled. Fortunately, gray squirrels have a habit of migrating in numbers when threatened with a food shortage, and they managed to survive despite the ruthless deforestation. Not only will squirrels migrate to a new area to find food, they will migrate in masses when their own numbers become too great. They have been known to swim great rivers during such migrations, despite the fact that they are poor swimmers and many drown while attempting to cross large bodies of water.

The gray squirrel *(Sciurus carolinensis)* is the best known of the squirrels, largely because he is the most abundant. This species, also known as bushytail or silvertail, is a mottled salt-and-pepper hue with lighter underbelly and face markings. An average-sized gray squirrel weighs about 1 pound and achieves an overall length, including the tail, of 18 or 19 inches at maturity. The tail is 8 to 10 inches long and is kept curled in a figure S over the animal's back when he is resting or feeding.

Gray squirrels mate in early spring, and the gestation period is about forty-four days. In the northern states the first litters—generally of two to four—are born in March or April. In the South the first litters may come as early as February. Two litters per season is average.

The gray squirrel is found from Maine to the Dakotas, south through central Texas and east to the Atlantic and Gulf Coasts, as well as in large areas of Canada. Throughout his range, the squirrel inhabits hardwood forests where he feeds on hickory nuts, acorns from oaks, butternuts, and beechnuts. He also eats the buds of elm and maple trees.

The gray squirrel, like other woods squirrels, doesn't hibernate, though he does retreat into hollow trees for periods of time. Despite this, he constantly gathers a supply of nuts. It is said that he forgets most of the places he buries his food, but if so, his work isn't wasted: the process serves to transplant tree seeds which otherwise wouldn't grow.

Two traits of gray squirrels indicate the best technique for hunting them. First, squirrels won't tolerate the noise and presence of people, and will retreat out of sight. Second, squirrels do the majority of their feeding and moving about just after daylight. Therefore, you should be in the woods *before* daylight, and you should hunt alone. If you do encounter other hunters in the area, head in the opposite direction. Wear camouflage clothing—say, mottled russet and dull green for fall days. Bright or colorful clothing spells danger to bushytail.

If you are hunting without a dog, you have the choice of either stalking or still-hunting. Still-hunting, as used in this book, means that the hunter remains in one place and allows the game to show itself and approach to within shooting range. In still-hunting squirrels, the hunter usually posts himself against the trunk of a large tree and waits. Often after minutes he will catch sight of a squirrel working in the high branches, or hear the sound of nuts hitting the ground. In a still forest this noise

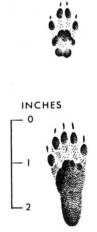

INCHES
0
1
2

Tracks of gray squirrel, forefoot (top) and hind foot.

Pattern of gray squirrel's tracks is a series of bunched prints. Hind feet register in front of forefeet.

is magnified, and the clattering can be heard for some distance. Sometimes the hunter may have to wait an hour or so in a cramped position. But his patience, assuming he is quiet and immobile, will eventually be rewarded. He will catch sight of old bushytail. When the squirrel stops, he carefully raises his rifle and shoots.

The preferred outfit for this type of still-hunting is a .22 rimfire rifle, usually equipped with a low-mounted scope of low magnification. Since squirrels are ordinarily shot at short ranges, some hunters use solid-point .22 ammunition. This will kill the animal and prevent ruining a lot of meat if the head shot happens to be a bit cornerwise, with the bullet going afterwards into the body. Many hunters refuse to use solids.

My friend Henry Rhyne, of North Carolina, likes a neck shot. He says it kills better and destroys less edible meat. In dressing the squirrel he removes the lower jaw, nose, and eyes, but leaves the rest of the head. It has a remarkably large brain which is quite a delicacy.

In the second method of hunting, the hunter moves *slowly* and *quietly* through a stand of woods, listening for the small noises of squirrels cracking nuts or moving among the leaves or branches, watching for a glimpse of the animals. This is the harder technique. A moving hunter is always easier for any game to see than a still-hunter when the game itself is moving. When the hunter spots a squirrel, the rifle should be carefully raised—actually inched into position, without moving the body—and the shot got off. A single gunshot seldom scares any game. Even several spaced shots will not frighten a gray squirrel as much as the sight of the hunter.

The enemies of the gray squirrel are the larger fast-flying hawks, horned owl, fisher, weasel, fox, bobcat, and wolf. In his treetop home, the squirrel has learned to outwit such enemies by two procedures. By jumping from branch to branch, and even from treetop to treetop, he can thwart such enemies as the four-footed fisher and bobcat. The second technique is even simpler—he simply runs to the opposite side of the tree trunk. An owl coming hard at a squirrel ascending or descending a tree is apt to bat his brains out on the trunk if he dives too long at the furry target, which flits around the tree at the last second.

Henry Rhyne has a trick to fool a squirrel that runs to the opposite side of the tree. He ties a string to a bush, then walks to the opposite side of the tree. After waiting several minutes, he shakes the bush with the string and the squirrel shows himself. He has to shoot quickly, as the squirrel doesn't stay fooled for long.

Another way the squirrel evades enemies is simply to lie flat on top of a high, outstretched limb. Because of his protective coloration, even the keenest eyes have a hard time spotting him in this position. Early settlers, who used large-caliber flintlocks, killed squirrels on tree limbs with a technique called "barking." They aimed just under the squirrel's heart and hit the bark of the limb, killing the squirrel with the shock of the bullet.

Shotgun hunters like to hunt squirrels as much as do rifle enthusiasts and argue that shooting them on the go with the scattergun is just as sporting. The question will never be settled, but many hunters do use shotguns, and often in conjunction with dogs. For this type of shooting, a good 20 gauge is almost ideal. It is light to carry and throws an adequate charge. A fine one for the purpose would be Winchester's Model 101 over-under with 28-inch modified and full barrels. It weighs just over 6 pounds.

Hunting squirrels with dogs is also a popular sport. John Phillips, a partner with whom I have hunted Alaska and the West many times, and who has hunted the bushytails all his life, described his method in a recent letter:

"Late in the season when the leaves are gone and most of the food is on the ground, it is real sport to hunt with a squirrel dog or treeing dog. I have found that most any dog with a little training will tree squirrels. However, some of the best known squirrel dogs are in the rat terrier and fox terrier class. I have, however, hunted with some very good German shepherd and regular shepherd dogs that made excellent squirrel dogs. A good squirrel dog will pick up the scent of the squirrel and trail it and tree it, but, as I said, most any dog will run one by sight and tree it. When hunting late in the season with dogs, I prefer using a .22 rifle; in the early part of the season I use a shotgun since most of the squirrels are moving then."

The fox squirrel *(Sciurus niger)* was so named because of his coloration. His upper body is a mottled gray, but his paws, face, underbody, and tail are reddish, similar to the coloration of the red fox. There are other color phases of this species, including melanism and albinism.

Our largest wild squirrel, the fox squirrel will reach 25 inches in length and weigh two and a half times as much as the gray squirrel. His bushy tail is almost as long as his body. In some regions he is known as the big red squirrel or the yellow-bellied squirrel.

The fox squirrel is found in far fewer numbers than the gray squirrel; in many regions where he was once quite abundant he is now extinct. Perhaps one reason for this is that he presented a larger target to hunters and was easier to hit than the gray squirrel. The largest remaining area of considerable fox squirrel population is in South Carolina.

The technique of hunting the fox squirrel is basically the same as for hunting the gray, or any other species of squirrel. Weapons used are the same. In areas of the country where handgun hunting is permissible, the fans of the short gun are coming to use scope sights for the sport. Damage to the squirrel population with the short weapon is slight, but there is quite a thrill to bagging a bushytail with a 6-inch barreled .22 revolver, scope-sighted single-shot pistol, or with a reduced load in a larger-calibered sixgun.

There are other lesser-known species of tree squirrels. One is the small red tree squirrel *(Sciurus vulgaris)*. This speedy little fellow is most ferocious, and oddly enough, one of his mortal enemies is the gray squirrel. The red will pursue the gray species and inflict many teeth wounds. The male gray's especially vulnerable spot is his scrotum and some observers swear that the red squirrel often purposely castrates the larger gray. Others claim that there is no especial intent on the part of the red, but that the scrotum of the larger, slower animal just happens to be a good target. In either case, many gray squirrels do become castrated in the process, though others are sterilized by a bot-fly infestation in the testes.

Small red squirrels are known in conifer country simply as "tree squirrels." In Canada and the West, they are the principal food of the tree marten. The marten is larger and captures the tree squirrel by sheer speed.

This little red squirrel is protected by law in some areas, but is shot in other regions of the North for his hide and for food. Like the gray and fox squirrel, he evades his enemies by sprinting along the ground, across logs and branches and up the boles of trees. He also knows the trick of keeping the trunk of a tree between himself and a hunter. The food of this species is usually conifer nuts.

A beautiful but little-known species which is protected by law is the Kaibab squirrel, found on the Kaibab Plateau in Arizona. This squirrel has black underparts, a huge silvery tail, and tufted ears and is comparable in size to the gray squirrel. While deer hunting in late fall on the Kaibab, I have seen them cavorting about, unmolested, at the campgrounds at Jacob Lake.

Prairie Dog

Richardson's Ground Squirrel

8

Prairie Dogs and Ground Squirrels

SQUIRRELS THAT burrow in the earth instead of living in trees are known as ground squirrels. One of the best known of this group is the prairie dog *(Cynomys ludovicianus)*. Other closely allied species are known, according to locality, as the chiseler, picket post, sod poodle, spermophile, and ground squirrel.

The average prairie dog grows to 14 inches in length, and this includes a 4-inch tail. The pelage is yellowish above and whitish below, with the outer third of the tail black.

These rodents live in colonies close to food supply in the arid country of the West. They usually can be seen sitting upright outside the network of holes and tunnels they dig in the earth. When a prairie dog senses danger, he gives a sharp, shrill whistle, warning the other members of the colony, who then disappear into their holes.

Prairie dogs and other ground squirrels normally feed on natural grasses and plants, but they prefer domesticated plants of man such as alfalfa, timothy, and the grain crops. When the source of food dwindles, the entire colony will move to another location and construct a new network of burrows and tunnels. In northern states they hibernate and emerge at about the same times as the rockchuck.

Ground squirrels begin mating in early spring, and the young are born in April and May. Litter size varies according to the species but averages from four to six.

Where no program of control exists, ground squirrels of all species multiply rapidly and do irreparable damage to agricultural lands. Texas at one time had such an infestation of ground squirrels that a program of mass extermination had to be put in effect. Recently, the infestation of such rodents in Wyoming has reached the point that many of the high ranges for domestic stock and elk were partially ruined.

Such ruination comes about because of the burrows. The rodents push up the earth into small mounds, forming a lacy network of loose earth. They either eat the grass or kill it by covering it with earth. Other larger animals such as the badger then enlarge the holes and use them. The mouths of the burrows are normally formed in such a way that rains can't enter. Periodic rains and the dew from green grasses and plants are sufficient water for these rodents, who can survive in areas completely devoid of lakes or streams. Enemies of ground squirrels include the badger, coyote, and rattlesnake, all of which can catch them in burrows or on the ground.

A good way to locate ground squirrels is to drive through desert regions which border outlying farmlands. Often where cleared fields border sagebrush lands a dike will remain at the junction. Ground squirrels like to burrow in these dikes and ridges, since no water can get down into their network of holes. Similar dikes within farmed lands will often be used by the rodents. Fencerows are also favored burrowing grounds. In prairie country or in grassy pasture lands, ground squirrels choose the higher knolls and dry mounds for their burrows. Unless disturbed by excessive shooting or lack of food, the little animals will use the same general locations from

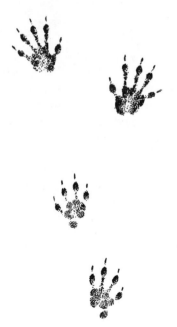

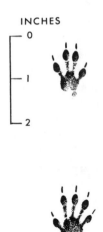

INCHES

0

1

2

Tracks of prairie dog, forefoot (top) and hind foot.

Prairie dog running in sandy soil. Tracks register in groups of four prints with 4 to 6 inches between groups.

INCHES

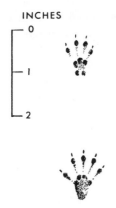

Ground squirrel tracks, forefoot (top) and hind foot.

Tracks of ground squirrel running in mud. Groups are more widely separated than those of prairie dog, usually 9 to 15 inches apart.

year to year. Once a good ground squirrel area is found, it may be used annually.

Perhaps the best procedure for finding prairie dog towns and other ground squirrel colonies is simply to ask farmers and ranchers in your area where to locate the animals. Sincerity and courtesy will always elicit honest information. When you want to hunt on private lands, be sure to ask permission. Hunting on such lands is not a right but a privilege granted by the landowner.

When a colony of ground squirrels is found, it is not a good idea to completely eliminate the pests from an area. A few of them are necessary to the ecology of the land. Large colonies should only be hunted to control their numbers.

Once you find a colony of rodents, patience is the key word from then on. The trick is to move so slowly that any squirrels alerted by your presence will run only to the edge of their burrows and stop instead of going below ground. That is a good time to shoot. Raise your rifle slowly, literally by inches, and get off a shot at a squirrel as he pauses. Once disturbed, the ground squirrel will retreat down his burrow. At this point, it's best to sit as low as possible, remain motionless, and wait. It takes patience, but eventually one or more animals of the colony will reappear and give you another chance for a shot. A good trick is to move on past the colony, then sit down and watch. Many a squirrel, thinking danger has passed, will come out of his burrow.

The .22 rimfire long-rifle cartridge, in a repeating rifle, is standard ground squirrel equipment. Sighted for about 60 yards, and scope-equipped, this combination is effective on ground squirrels up to 100 yards when used in the sitting position. Hollow-points should be used, to insure a clean kill.

The second hunting procedure requires precision equipment and greater shooting skill. Instead of using a .22 rimfire, use a fine long-range varmint outfit. Such varmint cartridges as the .22 WMR, .22 Hornet, .222 Remington, .219 Zipper, .223 Remington, .218 Bee, .224 Weatherby Varminter, and .225 Winchester are all good calibers for precision work. Usually such a cartridge will be chambered in an accurate

43

rifle wearing a scope sight of from 6 to 12 magnification and "tuned" to gilt-edge trigger-pull. With such an outfit, you can post yourself at a great distance from a ground squirrel colony and assume a solid prone position.

A fine intermediate cartridge, especially for the hunter who is limited in finances and doesn't care to reload, is the recent .22 WMR cartridge. This hot little number will shove a 40-grain bullet at the velocity of the original Hornet, and might well be dubbed the "poor man's varmint cartridge." In a good repeating rifle with a good scope it is nearly ideal for the ground squirrel hunter.

Often in good ground squirrel country the hunter can assume a full prone position, since the terrain is normally level or nearly so. In other cases a commercial bipod or handkerchief bipod comes in handy. The conditions are generally ideal for the Ormond Swing, described in Chapter 1.

One of the big attractions of the ground squirrel family for hunters is that they can get in an enormous amount of practice with rifle-cartridge combinations used on larger species. Bag limits on ground squirrels are usually generous or nonexistent. Also, the lowly ground squirrel is fast coming to the attention of serious handgun hunters who want to keep in practice when deer-sized targets are not in season.

FEATHERED VARMINTS

Crow

9

Crow

THE CROW *(Corvus brachyrhynchos)* is found throughout the world, and his history as a pest is as long as his scientific name.

Known by his jet-black coloration and raucous voice, the crow will average about 20 inches in overall length. Both sexes are alike in color, and both give voice.

Crows nest in all kinds of trees but prefer tall conifers. Their nests are of sticks and twigs, and are often huge. The female lays a clutch of from four to six greenish eggs mottled with brown. These hatch after an incubation period of eighteen days.

Crows normally nest in inland areas, and in a general way the birds are migratory. That is, during summers and the breeding season, they remain inland while the food supply lasts. In winter, when snow covers a major part of the food supply the birds migrate either to warmer climates or to the coastal regions where the ocean supplies the food. In summer crows eat a great variety of foods—corn, wheat, fruits, seeds, and the carcasses of small animals such as cats, rabbits, snakes, squirrels, and even northern seals. In winter such species as clams, scallops, and dead fish provide the black birds with food.

The crow is a voracious eater with a seemingly unappeasable appetite. His destruction of young corn, fruit, and young birds and eggs, especially those of waterfowl, has caused the black predator to be universally hated. Hundreds, even thousands of the birds will come to a field, and before leaving will destroy an entire crop. Similarly, they will attack a wide belt of nesting grounds for ducks and often destroy one-fourth or more of the eggs.

One habit of the crow has made him vulnerable to destruction—his habit of coming annually to roosting trees in a large concentration. Many such roosting trees have been dynamited, usually under governmental supervision, killing thousands of the birds in one blast.

During the daylight hours, the crow is less easily outwitted. One of the smartest wild birds, he is suspicious of everything that doesn't look right to him and cannily keeps out of danger. This inherent intelligence is conditioned further by the fact that he is constantly harried as a species and left without peace. Other enemies, besides man, are large hawks and the larger owls.

Because crows are ubiquitous and plentiful, they make sporting quarry for the small-game hunter, and they are hunted in every region of the continent except the colder northern areas.

In the hunting of any game there are two basic procedures: one is to pursue the quarry in his own habitat; the other is to let the game come to you. Crows are sometimes taken by the first method—by searching for the birds in outlying fields, along river courses, in timbered areas, or at the carcasses of dead animals. The jet-black form perched atop a dead tree or limb can be seen for nearly a mile, especially in clear air. And where there is one crow, there will be others. Study the stubble of mowed alfalfa or grain fields for signs of animated black specks; with a pair of binoculars, a necessary accessory for crow hunting, you'll be able to locate the birds. Often you will spot them sitting on the posts of a fencerow. Similarly, a study of the sky may reveal crows flying. This is an especially fruitful method during a seasonal migration of the flocks. Such birds will be flapping along in slow-flying formation and can be spotted when they light at resting areas. The noise of their *caw-cawing* can be heard for a considerable distance.

In this type of hunting, you must locate the birds, then stalk to within long-range shooting distance and conceal yourself. With a precision rifle-cartridge combination, you can pick them off. The hot .22-caliber cartridges such as the .222, .223, .224, .225, and .22/250, used in a rifle capable of minute-of-angle accuracy, with a scope of from 6 to 12 power, make good crow-sniping outfits. Shots at 200–400 yards are common, and a solid rest is needed at such ranges.

This type of sport is similar to chuck hunting since you have to make that one shot count. Other crows will fly at the shot, but if you stay concealed they will generally come back to feed or perch in the area. This is a lean but satisfying type of crow hunting.

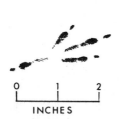

INCHES

Crow leaves a track about 3 inches long with 4 inches between prints.

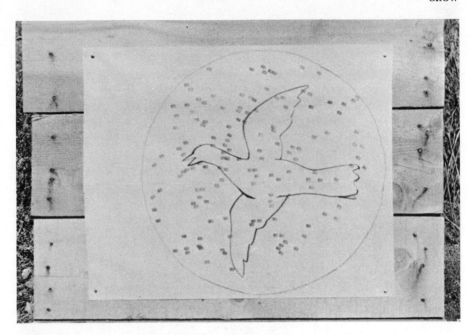

Patterning a shotgun for crow shooting helps to determine the best load for your gun. Here a fine pattern is thrown at 40 yards on a crow-sized target from a 12-gauge Mossberg pump gun with a variable choke set at modified, shooting No. 6 shot.

A far more thrilling and productive method is to employ the second hunting technique—and let the birds come to you. This means that you have to locate roosts, feeding places, or other areas of crow concentration; conceal yourself completely from the birds' sight, and bring them in with decoys of some sort.

The areas where crows concentrate usually have trees or foliage which you can use for concealment. Wearing camouflaged clothing helps. In summer or autumn, the mottled color of many commercial camouflage suits will match the foliage. Camouflage cloth, which is sold in 10-yard bolts, can be draped over a temporary framework of willows or brush to make a good shooting blind. For winter, wear white clothing such as carpenter's coveralls and cap, and conceal yourself in natural blinds of, say, corn shocks, or driftwood along a stream.

Artificial decoys can be used effectively by a concealed and camouflaged hunter. One of the best decoys is a stuffed owl, or imitation owl, perched naturally on a post. The crow hates his enemy the owl, and large numbers of the black birds will converge on the decoy and try to rip it apart. Artificial crow decoys are also effective perched in lifelike positions near the blind and at the appropriate places the live birds would normally choose—all within shooting range.

With the decoys set up, and live birds somewhere in the vicinity, you can use an artificial call. Some of the best crow calls are made by Olt and Popowski. Blown by an experienced caller, a call can bring in birds from great distances—they hear the call, spot the decoys, and come. It should be remembered that no crow call sounds natural of itself. It is simply an instrument. It has to be in the hands of someone who can simulate the natural call.

When the birds do come in, you can place the ones you shoot in lifelike positions on the ground, as extra decoys. The sound of shooting doesn't scare off the remaining crows for long. They will fly away, but they will come back. What does scare them is the sight of the hunter—you *must* stay concealed.

The best gun for this type of shooting is some kind of 12-gauge repeater using 7½, 8, or 9 shot. Peel a crow down and there's not much meat to hit. For this reason, fine shot and a big pattern are necessary.

Often in such shooting, dozens of crows will be killed in one location. In many an instance, a pair of concealed hunters at one roosting tree will almost burn their guns with fast, continuous shooting. For this reason, the dedicated crow hunter usually turns to handloading his own ammunition. Not only can he work up the best patterning loads for his particular gun, but he can save approximately 40 percent by reloading.

10

Owl

A COMMON characteristic of the owl is his dished, flattish face. The majority of subspecies have round faces; others have faces more oval in contour. The owl's eyes are set so they converge upon a single focal point, like the tubes of a double-barreled shotgun. He can see only one thing at a time, and instead of moving his eyes to change focal points, he revolves his head.

Owls are raveners and have sharp, curved beaks for tearing flesh, as well as strong, curved talons for grasping and holding small prey.

In North America there are literally scores of subspecies of owls. These range in size from the puny elf owl *(Micrathene whitneyi)* of the West, which is no longer than a man's hand, to the great gray owl *(Strix nebulosa)*, which has a wingspread of up to 5 feet.

Aside from vast differences in size, the differences in both color and markings are wide. The general coloration is a mottled mixture of drab gray, brown, and white, with the lighter tints occurring on the underbody. In combination, these colors camouflage the birds amid a great variety of surroundings.

Within this general coloration, however, there will be a pronounced barred marking such as in the barred or hoot owl *(Strix varia)*; the more speckled look of the western burrowing owl *(Speofyto cunicularia)*; and the nearly pure-white plumage of the snowy owl *(Nyctea scandiaca)*.

Both sexes of owls are alike in coloration; this wide assortment of markings being nature's way of matching protective coloration to habitat. In desert regions I have come upon small burrowing owls which could hardly be detected unless they moved.

Screech Owl

Great Horned Owl

INCHES

Tracks of the great horned owl in mud.

Similarly, I have watched Artic owls alight upon the windrows of pack ice, off Point Hope, Alaska. In that unending expanse of white, those white-hued owls were almost invisible. Even their dull-gray markings matched the irregular shadows.

The nesting habits of owls are as diverse as their species. Most owls, with the possible exception of the screech owl, are polygamous. They build their nests in old woodpecker or squirrel holes, old eagle or crow nests, in thick bunches of conifer limbs, or on the ground. Clutches of eggs usually number from two to seven and are often pure white.

Many species of owls are not only harmless to man but are actually beneficial. Their food consists largely of the small rodents which prey upon agricultural crops. In general the smaller owls are the most beneficial.

The larger species prey upon small game such as upland birds, rabbits, and squirrels. When this depredation occurs to the extent of endangering other species, it becomes necessary, in the interest of conservation, to keep the owls in balance with the rest of the wildlife population of the area. The three species which are most destructive to our small game—and therefore of most interest to the hunter—are the great horned owl, great gray owl, and hawk owl.

The trend today among conservation groups is to press for the prohibition of all hunting for owls. There is considerable debate about this among game management people, but an increasing number of states have passed laws against hunting. The legality of hunting them must therefore be constantly checked.

The hunting habits of the owls themselves are an indication of the best way to hunt them. Owls have keen eyesight, but cannot, as often supposed, see in utter darkness. They prefer to hunt at dusk, daylight, and during moonlit nights. They watch for prey from a tall tree or, in the case of a few species, swoop low over fields and spot moving prey from the air. When the owl spots a mouse, rodent, or small game bird, he swoops silently down, grasping for the prey with outstretched talons.

In hunting owls, then, you should move through deep woods where there are tall trees. Search the branches of these trees, especially the outstretched dry limbs which afford an owl a clear path for one of his downward swoops. Often owls will be chased out of the timber by their enemies the crows, and will perch in a tree removed from the crow area.

This means there is little opportunity to shoot at an owl with a shotgun. Instead, the rifleman will find his particular tool more useful, owing to the long range at which owls are generally spotted. A scope sight is useful, both for spotting and identifying a harmful species, and for the actual shooting.

Cartridges used for crows, chucks, coyotes, and similar-sized pests will be adequate for owls. These birds, however, are mostly feathers, so that often a shot you thought was "dead on" will get only a fluff of down. The birds are relatively hard to kill, so your shot must be well centered. If your first shot misses, an owl usually won't fly too far before perching again. Often this gives you time for a more careful stalk and a second shot.

11

Magpie

ONE MORNING just after sunup, I looked out of my office window and saw five magpies. Four of them were walking the grain stubble of the acreage in their characteristic high-stepping, twitching gait, picking up grasshoppers and other insects. The fifth was perched high atop a dry poplar tree 150 yards away. An example of the brotherhood which exists among this canny species, he was watching for more food —and for human enemies.

These birds have been doing this regularly since the grain has been cut. They have not been shot at, but there has been a considerable amount of shooting nearby, as I have been patterning shotguns and targeting rifles lately.

Had I moved as cautiously as possible out the back door, the birds would have flown, possibly back into the trees. Had I carried a *gun,* very probably the birds would have flown out of the field, or at least to the far end of the trees. Had I shot at one, at a range of 200 yards, all the others would have left the field for several hours.

This reveals several important characteristics of the magpie *(Pica pica).* The bird likes to be with his kind and to engage in a constant chatter of conversation. He is not entirely a predator but also gorges on insects, carrion, and the eggs of upland birds. And he is one of the smartest of wild birds, seemingly able to differentiate between a man with a rifle and a man unarmed. Indeed, among the winged predators, the magpie and the crow are the two species which man has been able to teach simple words.

The magpie is found from Alaska to the Southwest and as far east as Michigan, Ontario, Hudson Bay, and even Quebec. Many of the birds prefer to move into the

Magpie

Southwest for winter, though some are always seen in winter in the Northwest. I have seen them as far north as the Aleutian Islands in May, when snow still lay on the hills.

The magpie reaches a length of 21 inches and a weight of 5 ounces. The tail is long—over 11 inches in a full-grown bird—and tapers half its length. Conspicuous black and white markings identify the bird. I once had the rare privilege of seeing a brown and white magpie. In a lifetime in the outdoors, I have heard of only one other such bird.

Magpies nest in high trees or willows. Their nests are woven of small twigs and often lined with horsehairs. The female, which has the same pinto coloration as the male, lays from four to eight gray-brown eggs.

This bird is one of nature's most energetic scavengers, performing the beneficial

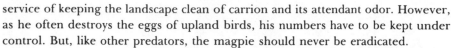

Magpie tracks in snow.

INCHES

service of keeping the landscape clean of carrion and its attendant odor. However, as he often destroys the eggs of upland birds, his numbers have to be kept under control. But, like other predators, the magpie should never be eradicated.

When a hunter kills a game animal a pair of wiskey jacks often will show up within minutes. These small birds will wait on a nearby tree limb, ready to carry off morsels from the offal after the hunter leaves. It is likely that the movement of these birds catches the eye of a high-flying magpie. He then investigates, cackles his find to others of his kind, and within hours the flocks of pinto scavengers are cleaning up the landscape. Their noise attracts the coyotes, who converge on the remains when the man scent dissipates. By this time, the odor of decaying flesh will have reached the nostrils of bears, and these animals also join the feast.

Thus, if you want to shoot magpies, you can expect to find them at the carcasses of dead domestic game or at the offal left by game kills. In rural areas, a sure way of bringing magpies around is to dump meat scraps or the internal organs of domestic chickens or game birds in a field or backyard. You should remain concealed as the birds come in.

Stockyards, too, are habitually visited by magpies. In areas where it is safe to shoot, you can conceal yourself within rifle range of such a yard, wait, and have one-shot shooting. You'll scare away the rest of the magpies with each shot, but be patient; within an hour or so they will reappear.

Old abandoned buildings and the trees surrounding them are good places to find magpies. When driving about in semi-settled country, you often will see the birds, which show up at great distances, perched in the tree tops or on the roof of the building. If you approach too closely, the birds will invariably fly off when you open the car door, if they haven't already been frightened off when the car stopped. A pair of hunters can often get a shot if one hunter keeps right on driving, while the other slips from the opposite side of the slow-moving vehicle and drops out of sight to a prone position.

Shooting magpies with a shotgun is great sport, but it is rarely possible because of the innate wariness of these birds. However, John Phillips and I once had an afternoon of such sport in the willowy brush along Wyoming's Shoshone River. The birds kept trading back and forth above the willow tops. Hidden in the same willows, we would quickly step out as one flew into range and let him have it. Small shot, 7½ or 8, in a 20-gauge shotgun makes for sporty shooting on this species.

The most effective outfit for magpies is a varmint rifle and cartridge which will shoot a bullet with precision accuracy at 3,000 feet per second and over. The rifle should be equipped with a scope of from 6 to 10 power. Good cartridges are the .222, .223, .224, .225, and .22/250. The ideal chuck rifle and cartridge is just right for magpies.

A Gallery
of Small Game Animals

**PRAIRIE
DOG**

WOODCHUCK

PORCUPINE

BEAVER

RED FOX

JACK RABBIT

COTTONTAIL RABBIT

RACCOON

COYOTE

BOBCAT

PREDATORS

Bobcat

12

Bobcat

THE BOBCAT *(Lynx rufus),* often called wildcat, is one of our most widely spread predators, ranging across southern Canada and south to Mexico and the Gulf states.

The bobcat's spotted coloration gives him camouflage in almost any terrain or foliage. His basic color is a pale tan heavily spotted and barred with black. His ears are tufted and his tail is rather short. The fur on his feet goes well down between his oversized toes, making it possible to run well on crusted snow. The bobcat's eyes are adjusted better than many species for seeing in all light conditions. In bright light the pupil is but a thin elliptical slit; but in poor light it becomes nearly round. This makes it possible for the bobcat to hunt well at night, though he does hunt during daylight hours as well.

An adult bobcat is about 36 inches long and weighs from 20 to 35 pounds—more in extreme cases. Bobcats mate without regard for season or area. From two to four young are born in caves, rocky ledges, or big hollow logs. Food consists of small animals—mice, ground squirrels, rodents, rabbits, domestic poultry, and even small deer.

Anyone who has watched a domestic cat stalk a mouse will understand the bobcat's method of hunting. The cat stalks soundlessly, close to the earth, pausing between successive short, quick runs. When close enough to his prey, he springs, grasps it in his long claws, and kills by biting into the neck and spine.

In rocky canyon areas of the West, bobcats are hunted by following the rim of a canyon, keeping out of sight as much as possible, and studying the opposite rim and bluffs. Binoculars, or a high-powered scope on the rifle, are helpful in locating the animals.

Winter is a good time for this type of hunting since there is apt to be more spoor to tell you if there are cats in the area. Veteran hunters, on finding fresh sign, sprinkle a few pounds of ground meat in the area and patiently wait across the canyon for the animal to appear.

In winter you can hunt bobcats along with snowshoe rabbits. Often snowshoes are needed for traveling in the heavy timber which the rabbits prefer at this time. When you come upon a fresh bobcat track meandering among the trees, a sign that the cat is hunting rabbits himself, follow the track, and often you'll be rewarded by the sight of a gray bobcat up ahead.

For both types of hunting a rifle is best, since bobcats usually can't be approached very closely. Any cartridge suitable for chucks, crows, or similar pests will be adequate for bobcats, if they are hit in the chest area. Cartridges like the .243 and .250 Savage are better.

A more thrilling form of bobcat hunting is coursing them with dogs. Again, winter is the best time to hunt, as the pelt is better then and snow makes the sport easier. Any dog inherently hates cats, so a wide variety of dogs and hounds are used. However, those species of hounds and dogs which will double on other species such as raccoon and cougar are generally best. Foxhounds are a preferred breed.

The technique is fairly simple. Take the dogs to bobcat spoor and turn them loose. They will cast about until they pick up a scent, then with a yowl begin the chase. Sometimes a bobcat will elude the dogs for miles. Sometimes the dogs will course the cat in a circle back towards the hunters. You can climax the chase by shooting the bobcat as he runs before the dogs, or let the dogs eventually catch the cat and kill him themselves.

Often the hounds will chase the bobcat a distance, then bring him to bay or chase him up a tree. The hunters then catch up and either dispatch the cat, rope it, or let him go.

The latest hunting method entails calling bobcats with an artificial predator call. The cry of a dying rabbit can, with practice, be simulated on an artificial call, luring the bobcat to collect an easy supper. This hunting technique was pioneered by a Mr. Burnham of Marble Falls, Texas. It is carried on by his two sons, Winston and Murray, who now manufacture a fine line of predator calls, and with whom I have hunted.

To utilize this method, you must conceal yourself in a natural blind of some kind

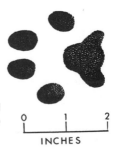

Tracks of the bobcat are more rounded than those of a dog or coyote. Claws do not register.

0   1   2

INCHES

—usually the local brush, which may be used as is or arranged so that it looks entirely natural. Camouflage clothing is a great help. The call of a wounded rabbit sounds something like *Ker-aaah! Ker-aaah!* It is rather high pitched and has a vibrato. Two calls are used. The first, usually deeper in tone and stronger, can be heard for a full mile on a windless day. Windy days are not good for calling. The call is repeated several times at intervals of five to ten minutes. The second call, which is lighter in tone, more whimpering, simulates the dying cry of the rabbit. If no cat comes within a reasonable time, move to another location at least a mile away.

The bobcat will come in as he hunts, sneaking up, a short rush at a time. When he comes into view, you can shoot him with a sniping rifle, handgun, or bow and arrow. Or you may only want to photograph him. All are thrilling.

You can also call bobcats in the black of night, but you need a couple of strong electric headlamps like the kind miners use. When the bobcat gets fairly close, say, within 75 yards, the beam picks up his eyes. Normally this will cause him to stop for several seconds, long enough to get off a shot. You must remain absolutely still.

The Burnham brothers told me that they have known of bobcats actually jumping on the concealed caller. I can't think of a more nerve-shaking experience than to have 40 pounds of wildcat sink about twenty long claws into my back some dark night. But no one can say such hunting is dull.

A final tip for the shotgun hunter who comes on a bobcat while hunting birds, squirrels, or rabbits. It's a good idea to carry a few shotgun slugs. These are accurate, and in 20, 16, or 12 gauge have plenty of punch for bobcats. Five-shots groups with these slugs at 50 yards will cover not over 3 to 4 inches, even when using the plain shotgun sights. I have one group, shot at a full 100 yards and off the bench with a 20 gauge gun, which covers just over 6 inches. Such a load is handy for the bobcat which would be just out of range of your No. 6's.

Hunter lugs a coyote back to his desert vehicle. Winter is best time for hunting this western predator—the pelt is prime and tracks are visible in the snow.

13

Coyote

THE COYOTE *(Canis latrans)* resembles a small gray wolf in appearance. Adults will run from 20 to over 40 pounds in some cases, and are characterized by a sharp nose, sharp-pointed ears, and a long flowing tail on the order of foxes. Coloration varies from a yellow-gray, to salt-and-pepper, to almost creamy white, with a tendency toward a thicker, whiter hue when prime in winter.

This species ranges from northern Alaska all the way to South America, with the greater numbers occurring in the prairie and western regions. It is often called the prairie wolf.

Coyote whelps are born in dens and average six to seven. There are cases on record where there have been more than twice that number of young.

Like the crow, the coyote has been harrassed unmercifully by man because of his liking for domestic poultry and sheep. He has been trapped, shot, coursed with hounds, and poisoned. Despite all this, the coyote has proved himself fit to survive, often right in man's back yard, and in many instances upon the food man provides. He has done this because of a superior wisdom and cunning in evading traps and poison, the ability to outrun any dogs except those bred especially for coursing, and a canny sense of impending danger.

Besides domestic fowl and stock, coyotes eat small rodents, offal, carrion, mice, birds, and especially rabbits. In the West, any large concentration of jack rabbits is a fair indication that coyotes may be near. Three or more of the little desert wolves will race a jack rabbit in relays, conserve their own strength by periodic rests until the rabbit tires, then close in for the kill.

The cry of the coyote is one of the most thrilling "tunes" of the wilds. The short, eerie *yip-yip-yip-yowoooooooo!* will be repeated by any other coyote in the area; and two coyotes, to the inexperienced ear, will sound like a full half-dozen.

There are many ways of hunting this cagey little wolf. Most hunters go after him in winter, since the prime pelt will bring them a few dollars to help pay expenses, or be a fine trophy. At one time, prime winter coyote fur would bring up to $25. Now, with the advent of nylon "fur," and a trend away from fur in women's clothing, the value of a hide has not increased much.

If you want to hunt coyotes, always be alert for them while after big game. They are seen more at sunup and dusk than at other periods of the day, and will often be spotted as they trot up open sidehills, along high game trails, and around the edges of large, open meadows where they catch mice. Tracks will indicate their presence —small, roundish tracks, quite like those of a small domestic dog.

When you see a coyote, the best bet is to get as low to the ground as possible, concealed where you can, and be prepared to shoot when the animal pauses. Unless he has spotted you he will move a short distance, then pause to look around.

A good way of hunting coyotes is to drive through desert areas in winter in a rugged four-wheel-drive vehicle equipped with chains and spot the animals as they move about hunting rabbits. Often it takes several hours of driving to locate a couple of the yodel-dogs.

Fairly deep snow and the month of February are a good combination for this kind of hunting. Fresh spoor shows up well in deep snow, and the snow slows down the coyotes and keeps them in one area. February is the mating month, hence the coyotes are a little less wary.

INCHES

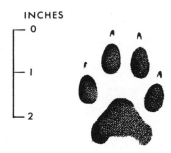

Tracks of the coyote. Note difference between imprint of heel pad of forefoot (top) and that of hind foot.

Two men make a good team; one drives, the other hunts. If the animal is watching —and this may occur at ranges of 300 yards or more—one hunter should get out of the vehicle on the side opposite the coyote and drop into a solid shooting position, while the driver keeps going.

When hunting in the desert, you should wear warm clothing—wool shirts, insulated pacs, warm pants and coat. Always carry sleeping bags along in the event of a break down and you have to camp overnight. A small supply of food, for emergencies, should always be carried in the vehicle. Binoculars are a must.

The best coyote outfits are similar to the best rifle-cartridge combinations for rockchucks. Rifles should be superbly accurate and equipped with scopes of from 4 to 8 power. Cartridges should shoot bullets in excess of 3,000 foot-seconds. Here are some good ones:

Cartridge	Bullet	Velocity
.22/250	55 grains	3800 fs
6 mm. Remington	80	3500
.243 Winchester	80	3500
6.5 mm. Remington Magnum	120	3000
.25/06 Remington	87	3400

Larger calibers such as the 7 mm., .270, .280, .264 Magnum and even 7 mm. Magnums, when using lighter bullets, make fine coyote rifles; so do wildcats with comparable ballistics.

In the more open rolling hills and prairies, coyotes are often hunted with snow-planes. These are air-driven vehicles which run on three large skis in tricycle arrangement, and are powered by a rear-mounted airplane motor and prop. They hold two men. In deep snow hardened by crust, these little planes can make 70 miles per hour or more, and can run down any coyote caught in open country. A 12-gauge shotgun is the preferred weapon for this thrilling sport.

Since the advent of the snowmobile, the snowplane is losing ground as a coyote runner. The little two-man power toboggans, mentioned for wolf-hunting, can run on snow of any condition because of their endless, cleated drive-belt which contacts the snow itself. The higher-powered models can make up to 40 miles per hour and over, and can negotiate timbered country as well as open areas.

In the open desert and prairie country, coyotes also are hunted from light aircraft. Winter is the best time, as the animals show up against the white snow.

Good places to hunt coyotes in the fall are near the offal left at game-kills. In wilderness country, coyotes will habitually come to game-kills after twenty-four hours have passed and the man-scent has gone. If you approach a game-kill from *above,* and from the opposite direction from which the hunter left the kill, you're apt to spot a coyote.

In forested country containing many game or horse trails, coyotes tend to follow such trails on their hunts. The coyote seldom looks above him for danger and the hunter can turn this trait to his own advantage. I know several old woodsmen who delighted in sitting high in a conifer tree at dusk or daylight and shooting a coyote moseying along the trail beneath.

In outlying ranch areas near timber country, where stacked hay remains in the meadows after it is cut, coyotes come into a meadow, usually at dusk and daylight, to hunt for mice. If you climb on top of one of the high stacks just before daybreak and conceal yourself in the loose hay, you'll get a shot at coyotes—if they're in the area. One thing to watch is the magpies. If a magpie, flying out to the meadow at daylight to feed, spots the hunter on the stack, he'll cackle in alarm; and the coyote, moving from the timber and watching the bird, will turn quickly and be gone. Since using such poisons as 10–80 on coyotes has been banned in many parts of the country, the wily animals have increased in number. They pose a danger to many game herds but are a boon to the varmint hunter. For all his faults, the coyote deserves a better death than from slow poisoning.

Coyotes can be called in with an artificial predator call that simulates the sound made by a wounded rabbit. The best time for this is on a calm evening at dusk. Dress yourself in camouflage clothing and get into some form of natural blind from where you can see in several directions. Unlike the bobcat, which comes in cautiously, the coyote normally comes in at a run. His style of hunting is to use his speed to overtake the wounded rabbit.

14

Gray Fox

THE GRAY fox *(Urocyon cinereoargenteus)* is a dainty-looking little predator which resembles a miniature coyote. Like the coyote, he has a pointed nose, erect ears, and a long, flowing tail. Adults will average around 8 to 10 pounds in weight. The back and sides, as well as most of the tail, are a salt-and-pepper gray mixed with buff. Underparts are grayish white; the tail tip is dark gray, almost black in appearance.

The range of the gray fox overlaps that of the red fox in many areas, but the gray likes the warmer climates of the temperate areas of North America and favors the rocky, brushy, and forested areas. Areas of the most population include a western strip within the boundaries of California, Nevada, and Oregon; a region at the four-statection of Utah, Colorado, Arizona, and New Mexico; an area from central Texas across the Mississippi Valley (with the exception of Mississippi State) to the Great Lakes and over the Northeastern states.

This fox feeds on small rodents, moles, small birds, berries, grapes, nuts, crayfish, and insects. He also kills young domestic lambs when possible. The young are born in dens, from two to four or more in a litter, and these stay inside the den for over a month. Mates are more monogamous than many other species, and both male and female bring food to the den for the young.

Two diseases are carried by the gray fox which are harmful to man—tularemia and rabies. Like the grouse and varying hare, the gray fox is cyclic, with years of great abundance and years of relative scarcity.

The most popular method of hunting the gray fox has always been with dogs. The

Gray Fox

INCHES

Tracks of gray fox, forefoot (top) and hind foot.

best breeds are the various foxhounds, including such breeds as the Black and Tan, Triggs, and Walker hounds.

The hounds are taken to a likely area and turned loose. They cast about until the scent of a fox is located, then are off trailing and baying. As the trail gets hotter, the noise and speed increase until the hounds catch up to the fox. Generally the gray fox won't give the prolonged chase that the red species will, but prefers to "tree" after a relatively short run. The rough country in which the gray is hunted may have something to do with this.

One of the gray fox's tricks is to head for impenetrable cover to slow down the hounds. He then zig-zags back and forth, much as a rabbit doubles back and forth when hard-pressed by dogs. This leaves an erratic trail, and by the time the hounds have unraveled it, the fox is away and into another mass of foliage. Eventually the animal is brought to bay—either in a tree or a den hole.

If, according to tradition, the hunter does not kill the fox, and the hounds themselves can't catch him, he is allowed to get away. Generally it is against tradition in the South to shoot a chased fox. In the North, hunters usually shoot the quarry.

The gray fox is particularly easy to deceive with a well-blown varmint call, owing to his natural greed for rabbits. The best time is just after dark, when the fox himself is out hunting. Two hunters work as a team—one is equipped with a powerful electric headlamp; the other does the calling and the shooting. The hunters conceal themselves in a natural blind with a good view for about 40 yards all around. The area should have sparse brush through which the fox can approach. The caller simulates the cry of a dying rabbit—usually the squeal of the cottontail—repeating it at intervals to give the fox time to approach. Then the caller blows the second call —a dying whimper.

During the calling, the other hunter shines the headlamp over the terrain. The light should not be directed fully at the ground between the hunters and where game may come in, but just so its lower edge crosses the brushy cover. If the light is not beamed directly at an incoming fox, it doesn't seem to alarm him unduly. Eventually, with luck, the beam will pick up the fox's eyes. The hunters must now remain perfectly quiet. The signal to be ready comes when the lamp man turns the beam to a central focus and beams it directly down on the fox, who is generally standing still at this point, listening. If the animal is within range, the hunter shoots. Depending on that range, he uses either a rifle or a shotgun.

Red Fox

15

Red Fox

THE RED fox *(Vulpes fulva)* is the best known of the North American foxes. He is the Reynard of children's literature and the hero of many of Aesop's fables, the object of that grudging admiration with which man has always regarded an animal he cannot entirely outwit.

There are three reasons why the red fox is better known than the gray fox: he has a far greater distribution; he is more colorful in hue; his open habitat gives the hunter with hounds a far more exciting, uncertain chase.

This fox is yellow-red in general color and runs to over 3 feet in length. One-third of this length is tail. The red species has sharp ears, pointed nose, and slanted eyes comparable to the gray fox, but will average a bit more in weight. The average adult weighs about 10 pounds.

The young are born in dens, often a network of rocky apertures, dug holes, or the appropriated burrows of the badger or other burrowing animals. There are usually around five in a litter. The vixen remains inside the den or close to it until the young emerge at somewhat over a month.

The red fox ranges from the Atlantic to the Pacific, and from the Arctic to the northern edge of Mexico. He prefers the wooded regions within this wide range, but is found more in the open areas than is the gray fox.

Food of the red fox consists of mice and ground squirrels, birds, rabbits (particularly cottontails), domestic poultry, and fruits including the grapes of the fables. Insects, too, form a part of the diet, as do small snakes.

The cunning with which the red fox outwits hounds has become legendary. He jumps from rock to rock, leaving scanty spoor. He doubles back. His speed is comparable to that of his pursuers. He matches all this with great stamina and a seeming delight in outrunning pursuers.

Because of the red fox's speed, wits, and endurance, he is hunted largely with dogs or hounds. In some areas fox hunting is so traditional that hunting clubs are formed. Large acreages are leased for hunting, and packs of hounds are bred over many years for the sport.

The hunter who owns several Walker, Triggs, or other good breed of foxhound can hunt on his own. When snow is on the ground is a good time, as visual spoor helps in locating an animal. The dogs course the animal until it runs before the hunter, or until they bring it to bay. It helps to be familiar with the hunting area, to know the runways and crossings a fox will habitually use. The hunter posts himself at such spots.

For shooting foxes coursed past the hunter by hounds, the favorite gun is a 12-gauge shotgun using express or magnum loads and No. 2 or 4 shot.

Rifle hunters, too, find fox hunting thrilling, and often score on a fox which moves about farmlands and open fields, especially after snow has fallen. The hunter moves along the fringe of trees or timber, staying concealed and watching for the animal to move into the open. Dusk is the preferred hunting time. Any good cartridge for use on crows, chucks, and similar pests is good for foxes, from the .22 WMR on up. The .222 Remington in a scope-sighted rifle is a fine combination.

INCHES

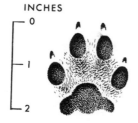

Tracks of red fox, forefoot (top) and hind foot. Hair between the heel and toe pads often shows in deep snow or mud.

16

Lynx

In MANY respects, the Canadian lynx *(Lynx canadensis)* looks like an enlarged version of the bobcat. The thick fur is similar in general coloration, a grayish-buff lightly spotted with varying shades of gray, but the tail is black only at the top of the guard-hairs and outer tip and is shorter than the bobcat's. His ears are longer and more tufted, and his face has a bit more ruff about its edges, as though he were peering from a hairy parka hood.

Adult lynxes will weigh up to 40 pounds or so. Like the bobcat, his feet are large for his body and fur-webbed for traveling on top of the snow. The imprint of a lynx's track in medium-hard snow resembles a small saucer. The individual toe definitions are hazy.

The young are born in dens in rocky ledges, caves, and heavy thickets occurring in rock formations. Two kittens make up a litter.

The lynx does most of his hunting at night, his food consisting of mice, small birds, spruce grouse, ptarmigan, and snowshoe rabbits. The snowshoe rabbit is first on his menu, and on hard snow the speedy lynx can catch the hare. Here again is an example of the cyclic relationship between predator and prey. In years of snowshoe rabbit abundance, there will be a big lynx population; in years of snowshoe rabbit scarcity, there will be a corresponding lack of lynxes.

The hunting methods used for this species are the same as those used successfully for bobcats—locating and chasing the animal with dogs. Winter is the best time for then the skins are prime, and lynx skins make beautiful trophies.

Actually, the Canadian lynx is not hunted too much. His habitat is remote from

Canadian Lynx

the large population centers and much of it is inaccessible in winter to the average hunter. Because of the physical difficulties involved, the majority of lynxes are either trapped or shot by professional trappers who are equipped to travel in the North country.

The little snowmobiles mentioned previously may change this to quite an extent. Currently, groups are being formed to take expeditions far afield from the urban centers, turning winter from a time to be endured to a season eagerly anticipated. This, and the increasing settlement of Canada and Alaska, may popularize lynx hunting as a winter sport. Certainly as the ratio of hunters to other more accessible game increases the lynx is going to become a more attractive quarry.

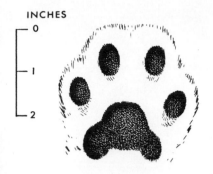

INCHES

0

1

2

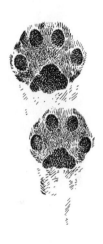

Lynx tracks in snow, forefoot (top)
and hind foot.

Pattern of lynx tracks in snow.

OTHER
SMALL
GAME

Raccoon

17

Raccoon

BEFORE THE white man settled in America, the Indians had long hunted the raccoon *(Procyon lotor)* for both his meat and his hide. They had given him a name which, roughly translated, means an animal that scratches with its hands.

The raccoon is a squat, short-legged animal which weighs on an average between 14 and 20 pounds. There are numerous subspecies, some of which weigh twice that amount. Three of the raccoon's most distinguishing characteristics are a sharp-pointed nose, a black face mask, and a ringed tail which is half the animal's body length and is responsible for his nickname "ringtail." The raccoon's pelage varies from gray-black to gray-brown to yellowish-gray, and the thick fur makes him look more bulky than he really is.

The normal range of the raccoon was once from the St. Lawrence River southward to the Gulf of Mexico and Florida, and from the Atlantic to the Mississippi. Like the moose, which migrated northward in search of new woods habitat, the raccoon moved westward. I saw my first raccoon in an abandoned orchard in the Minidoka country of southern Idaho and more recently have seen a considerable number of dead raccoons along the highways of the hill country of Texas, victims of passing automobiles. Plantings have been made in Alaska's southwestern area, and the animals are catching on. The success of these migrations and plantings depend on the animal's acceptance of a varied and often different food supply. While classed as a carnivore and being fond of such foods as crayfish, fish, frogs, and insects, the raccoon is equally fond of fruit, domestic corn, and other grain.

The favored resting spots and dwellings of this animal are hollow trees and ledges.

They are prolific, though not to the degree that rabbits are. Mating occurs during January and February, with litters of three to six young after a gestation period of just over two months.

The raccoon searches for food during the night and holes up during the day, normally in forested country, wastelands, or ledge areas near forests and brush. This nocturnal behavior dictates the best method of hunting him—with dogs.

The dogs used for raccoon hunting may be divided into two groups, coonhounds and coon dogs. Some of the better known hounds bred for the purpose are the English coonhound, Walker, Bluetick, Redtick, Redbone, Black and Tan, and Plott. Coon dogs may include the standard breeds and even dogs of more democratic ancestry. Often a prized coon dog may be just a mutt with an obsessive desire to sniff out a ringtail and scare him up a tree.

A good coon dog or hound reaches his prime at six years of age. This fact alone indicates how long it actually takes to focus such a dog's interest solely on raccoons and to train him to unravel this quarry's deceptive tricks. Many a good dog's future as a cooner has been cut short because he couldn't resist chasing deer, bobcats, or other game he sniffed on a night's hunt, instead of sticking entirely to raccoon.

If the course of a nocturnal coon hunt were followed during daylight hours, it would not be nearly so rugged, hazardous, uncertain, or exciting. Part of the great

INCHES

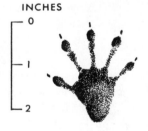

Raccoon tracks in mud, forefoot
(top) and hind foot.

Pattern of raccoon tracks.

thrill of coon hunting lies in these hazards and uncertainties, and the general spookiness that comes with night.

Two or three hunters with two to four coon dogs make a suitable party for a raccoon hunt. The hunter should be equipped with tough clothing to withstand the rigors of brush and rocks. Of equal importance is a good flashlight with plenty of spare batteries. Depending on the laws or customs of the particular area, guns may or may not be taken along.

The dogs are taken on leash to a point where raccoon spoor is apt to be found, or where the game itself can be encountered. In the northern tier of states, forested areas, creek courses, and edge country where forests meet marginal farmlands are all likely areas to hunt. In the South, swamps, mangrove regions, and agricultural lands which border such foliage are good spots. Abandoned farms, fields of corn, and lands which have reverted back to brush are good coon country. These areas should be located in advance, during daylight hours. When the dogs reach a likely area, they are turned loose. What happens then is quite like tightening the surcingle hand, nodding to the gate man, and taking off on a bronc out of gate number 5. The participant never knows which direction he is going or if he can stay on until he gets the prize. Such a hunt often lasts all night.

Raccoons are among the most intelligent of small game and have a perplexing bag of tricks. At the bay of the hounds upon their tracks, they may run, turn abruptly, and double back; swim a creek or stream; run a thin rail fence for several rods, then jump off and scamper away a right angle; spring from rock to rock, where the remaining scent will be sparse; or climb a tree.

Even when the raccoon has climbed far up a tall tree beyond the reach of the dogs, there is no certainty of his capture. From this elevated perch, he is apt to play one of his cleverest tricks—jump out of the tree, hit the ground with a soft thud which is covered by the noise of the hounds and be off and running again. There is nothing to do then except take up the chase once more.

Once the dogs successfully hold a raccoon until the hunters arrive, the coon's eyes may be "shone" with the flashlight, allowing one of the hunters to shoot the treed animal and end the hunt. Or one of the more athletic hunters may shinny up the tree and shake him out for the dogs. At this, there will be a fight. A big boar coon can lick an average-sized dog, especially if the coon can get the dog in the water, and some vicious battles often occur. One of the coon's favorite holds is to get the dog by the tender nose.

There has recently been legalized in some areas of the South what is called the "shake" season on raccoons. During that particular season, guns can't be used on treed coons, but the animals may be shaken out of trees for the dogs to kill.

Again, the dogs may be tied in advance of the "shake," to allow the animal to make another run. If the hunters wish to preserve their own sport in an area of scanty raccoon population, they may allow the animal to escape. If the dogs happen to put up two animals or an entire family, only one may be killed. As with other forms of hunting, killing the quarry is secondary to the excitement and suspense of the actual hunt.

Since much of the raccoon's habitat occurs in regions where roads intersect, and since there is no deterring a good cooner once on hot scent, many prized dogs are

Shaken from a tree by one of the hunters, a raccoon puts up a violent battle with a coon dog. The dog often gets the worst of these fights.

lost by getting hit by passing automobiles. An effective safety precaution is a dog collar with a bright-orange flourescent covering which shines in the beam of a headlight—much like a highway reflector. This will help motorists spot a passing dog in time to avoid hitting the animal.

Another gadget of great help to older coon hunters especially is a set of metal climbing steps. These are screwed into the bole of a big tree which hasn't climbable branches, enabling the hunter to shinny up the tree and shake out a treed raccoon.

18

Skunk

THIS OBNOXIOUS animal carries his own system of weaponry and communication, which not only advertises his presence but staves off most enemies in advance. Occasionally a great horned owl or a domestic dog will take on a skunk in battle. Both usually regret it.

The skunk carries his vile odor in a gland and expels it through the anal vent. The mist permeates everything in the proximity, and the smell is revolting to man and beast. It will even cause temporary blindness.

The best-known skunk is perhaps the striped skunk *(Mephitis mephitis)*. There are, however, approximately thirty subspecies, differing only in such characteristics as the white striping or spotting. Some of these are the Canada, Arizona, California, Great Basin, Puget Sound, Rocky Mountain, and swamp skunks. The basic marking of most skunks is a black body with the back and tail striped or spotted with white. There are differences in size depending on region and food supply. A full-grown skunk weighs from 6 to 8 pounds and is about 2 feet in length. He has a long, bushy, striped tail which, when erected, looks large in comparison to his body. There is overlapping of the species, but skunks of some subspecies are found over most of the United States and Canada.

Skunks eat rats, mice, the eggs of domestic fowls and wild birds, and are especially fond of young birds. They also eat frogs, lizards, and insects. Once accustomed to the eggs and young chicks of domestic poultry, skunks prey heavily upon them and are found around farmyards. In natural foliage, they prefer the brush of dikes, willow patches, trees bordering streams, and generally brushy waste areas. If any skunks are

Striped Skunk

INCHES

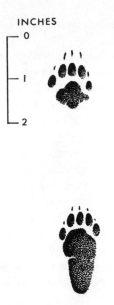

Tracks of striped skunk, forefoot
(top) and hind foot.

Pattern of striped skunk tracks.

in the area, you may be sure they will find fish heads which anglers toss out as garbage. Indeed, my first introduction to a skunk was at 3 o'clock one morning on the willowy bank of the Lost River. I awoke to find one sitting on my sleeping bag and eating a fish head I'd left in the garbage. I moved slightly, and the skunk moseyed in stately dignity off into the willows. I was lucky he didn't raise his tail and shoot me in the eye.

Skunks are especially fond of digging holes, often under old buildings, in which they spend the daylight hours. Once into such a hole, skunks are hard to get out. They stay during the day when they could be hunted and shot, but emerge when it is too hard to see. Daybreak is a good time to hunt a skunk which has burrowed under an abandoned building. Skunks move about more at that time.

Daybreak is also a good time to hunt skunks in their brushy habitat. They will often be seen moving alongside a brushy dike or fencerow, or near sparse cottonwoods bordering a stream. Occasionally, anglers floating a river will come upon skunks searching for food between the brush of the river bank and the gravel of the stream bed.

Poultry yards which have been raided by a skunk are good places to hunt. While the tracks and damage are still fresh, take a strong flashlight at dusk or daybreak and conceal yourself near the yard. The skunk that did the damage may very well return.

A .22 hollow-point rimfire cartridge is large enough for a skunk if the bullet hits the brain or heart area. A wounded skunk, however, will normally release his foul-smelling spray before he dies, so it is a good idea to make your first shot count. The

.22 WMR is a far better cartridge for this species. In a handgun with a 6-inch barrel, good sights, and crisp trigger-pull it is particularly effective.

An even better outfit for skunks is the combination, two-bore Savage Model 24 rifle-shotgun, adapted to the .22 WMR in the top barrel, and a 20-gauge shotgun tube below. For brush shooting it's best to set the firing mechanism for the shotgun barrel. If the skunk flushes at close range, or is come upon suddenly, the shot charge will kill it. If there's time for a long-range shot, the rifle part of the combination will be good out to 150 yards.

Hunters and trappers who have had wide experience with skunks have found ways to avoid much of the animal's odor. Some skin them under water. Others know how to handle the carcass to keep the scent inside the gland. Some cut out the entire gland before attempting to skin the beast. But if you handle a skunk which has not been surgically descented you will get some of the odor on you. Then you must wash your skin with strong soap and water. Burying contaminated clothing will help to remove the scent, if the ground is wet. It's safer to shoot a skunk, make sure he's dead if it requires a second shot; then forego the hide and leave without going too close. If any scent does get on shoes or clothing, the only complete cure is to burn them.

A further word of caution is in order. Years of severe drought produce a sharp increase in skunk populations and usually an increase in the cases of rabies among people who have been bitten by the animals. This is another reason for not getting too close to skunks. Because of the value of the pelt, the skunk is protected in many regions as a fur-bearer—especially in the northern tier of states. Many a hunter has remained a sweeter-smelling person for respecting this classification.

19

Wolverine

THE WOLVERINE *(Gulo luscus)* has long been a legend in the North country for his fighting ability and his extraordinary cunning in robbing traplines and despoiling food caches.

Also known as the "carcajou," and with less affection as the "glutton," the wolverine is a rather squat animal which reaches 3 feet in overall length, including the tail, and weighs up to 35 pounds. The coat is deep brown, almost black in color, with two lighter brown-tan stripes running the full length along the sides. The legs are rather short, and the animal runs in a short-strided "humpy" movement. From the distance, the wolverine often is mistaken for a small bear.

Range and distribution of the wolverine has been diminished in the northern tier of the United States by deforestation and civilization. At the present time, the wolverine's range extends over most of Canada coincident with the timber belts, and throughout most of Alaska south of the tundra.

An occasional wolverine is sighted in the northern part of the Northwest. Several years ago, as one example, a cattleman in the Lemhi area of Idaho near the Bitter Root Divide described for me an animal he'd seen in the pines there. I have no doubt that it was a wolverine. About 15 miles from where this is being written, a Wolverine Creek, flowing into the Snake River, tells of the animal's once being this far south.

Because of the animal's great stealth, cunning, and generally nocturnal habits, he keeps out of the sight of his enemy, man. Instead, the animal quickly ascertains the presence of man in an area, then proceeds to aggravate him by following his traplines and killing and ruining all game found in the traps. His powerful, stocky body with

Wolverine

INCHES

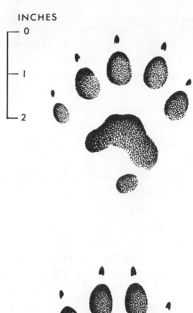

Tracks of wolverine, forefoot (top) and hindfoot. They resemble wolf tracks except wolf's have four toes, heel pads are different.

Pattern of wolverine tracks. Animal leaves a winding trail, indicative of inquisitive nature.

steel-like muscles, and his powerful jaws, make him a most formidable fighter. The wolverine's fight is always to the death, and he is seldom defeated.

Worse, the wolverine systematically raids the caches of food which northern trappers store during the summer months. As his nickname implies, he gorges on all he can eat; then he despoils what is left by excreting a foul-smelling fluid from glands at the anus over food, clothing, and gear.

Such despoilation has infuriated trappers and other woodsmen for decades, and they constantly swear to get revenge by trapping or killing the offender. But since wolverines are rarely seen, they can't be reduced by shooting. And this animal, above all others, is a natural master of stealing the bait from traps, tripping the steel devices without being caught.

It is said that very few outdoorsmen ever get to see a live wolverine, but I have been fortunate to have twice seen the animal in his natural habitat.

In 1961 John Phillips and I were returning from his brown bear kill in the

Aleutians, where we had been photographing and measuring the animal. Don DeHart and Fred Fredericks, outfitter and guide, had finished the skinning and were lugging in the hide on a packboard, a mile behind. Suddenly, across the creek bed, containing at this May season only gravel and driftwood, a smallish brown form came loping easily along, like a small brown dog. The gait was slow, and the beast would abruptly stop here and there, to investigate the short bush and brush interspersed in the driftwood patches. We stopped, partly hidden by the salmon berry bushes, and watched the animal until it disappeared from view. It was a wolverine.

Again in 1963, Herb Leake and I were hunting rams in Alaska's Little Tok River country. As we returned to camp through the inevitable bush, short Arctic birch, and dwarf spruce, Herb reined in sharply, and pulled his .300 Savage from the boot. Not over 50 yards ahead of us, a full-grown wolverine bounced in his peculiar humpy movement through the sparse bush and into a knot of spruce. The noise of the horses had evidently spooked it at close range. I believe Herb could have got off a shot at the animal, but being the gentleman he is, he waited to see if his guest could get a quick shot instead.

Another wolverine encounter was described to me that same year in the Yukon by Phil Neuweiler and his wife Cecelia. While hunting Dall Rams near Kluane Lake, Phil spotted something moving in the Arctic birch far up the mountainside. Putting the 20-power spotting scope on it, he discovered two wolverines viciously battling. Forgetting the rams, he steadied the scope and watched.

"Never have I seen such a wicked battle. They'd roll and claw and bite like tomcats. The fur, great hunks and strips of it, would fly—you could see it plain in the scope. Ceil and I watched for twenty minutes, in sheer awe. You never saw anything so vicious. The funny part, all they seemed to be killing each other about was some kind of big bone . . . and after they got through fighting, the one that licked the other left the danged thing laying there."

Phil, who has hunted all over the continent, told me he'd never seen such a wildlife spectacle.

To thwart the predatory and befouling habits of this animal, trappers and hunters who must store food and supplies in bush country construct a peculiar type of cache. Four tall spruces growing together in a clump are cut off at about 15-foot height. On these posts a flat platform of lumber, puncheon, or even 5-inch spruce poles are laid and fastened down. This platform extends far out beyond the four post tops in all directions. On this platform a tiny hut is built, roofed over to shed rain, and a door which may be locked is installed. For temporary use, plastic neoprene is now being used instead of the hut and simply folded over the gear and lashed down. Food is carried into the cache by means of a ladder, which is taken down and hidden in the brush afterward. If a wolverine climbs up one of the posts, he can't reach or jump out far enough to grab the edge of the platform and climb upon the cache. Whenever possible, the legs are made bear- and wolverine-proof by nailing tin around them —the tin usually coming from old 5-gallon gas cans.

If there is any possible way to hunt a wolverine successfully, it is to watch the area around a loaded cache in early morning or late evening. Otherwise, just keep alert

Cache in the North country to prevent wolverines from raiding food supplies.
Ladder is removed when hunters leave campsite.

while hunting other species in the animal's range—and perhaps you'll see a wolverine. You'll have to depend on the rifle-cartridge combination you are using at the time, but anything that's right for wolves, coyotes, or bobcats is large enough to kill a wolverine.

Porcupine

20

Porcupine

THE PORCUPINE *(Erethizon dorsatum)* is a squat, slow-moving animal which somewhat resembles a beaver but is smaller in size. An adult porcupine will reach 30 to 40 pounds in weight when very fat, but will drop to 15 or 20 pounds when poor. The animal achieves a length of 3 feet, of which 8 inches or so is tail. Tracks of an adult porcupine are quite like those of a cub bear, especially when seen in snow.

The porcupine's quills are his most pronounced characteristic. These are sharp, black-tipped, hollow spines of pale yellowish color protruding from all over the animal's back and tail. During normal movement these quills do not show to their fullest length, since they are partially hidden by the animal's brown-gray fur undercoat. But when the animal is alerted or angered he erects these quills, making him appear like a big animated pin-cushion.

The range of the porcupine includes most of the forested area of Canada, the northeastern part of the United States, and the Rocky Mountain country as far south as Mexico. Food includes most green material—tree bark, twigs and small plants.

Porcupines mate during late winter or early spring, with two being an average litter of young.

The porcupine is a slow mover, but his quills provide a built-in protection. These quills not only are sharp and painful to the flesh of other animals, but they are constructed on the order of fish hooks. Along their length are tiny barblets, pointing backward along the stem. Once the quill is driven into the flesh of an animal, it does not come out easily and will drive deeper and deeper.

Domestic dogs can't seem to learn not to tangle with a porcupine. A dog often tries to bite the animal, and is rewarded by a noseful of quills. Then it is necessary to hold the dog and pull all the quills out—a very painful process. Nevertheless, the next time the dog meets a porcupine, he'll invariably repeat the mistake. To remove quills from a big, strong dog, it's generally best to tie both pairs of feet together, then hold the dog suspended upside down, with a pole between the tied feet. There is less danger of being bitten with the dog in this position, and it is easier to remove the quills. Often a coyote or bear bites a porcupine and gets a mouthful of quills. Unable to get them out, the animal often dies of slow and painful starvation.

The porcupine does a lot of damage to forests and orchards, mainly by girdling trees. He generally prefers conifers, and within a few weeks can girdle and ruin a dozen or more huge trees. He likes domestic trees as well. Several years ago, an adult porky came in winter to our orchard and before anyone had noticed him, he'd climbed, barked, and half ruined a prized Delicious apple tree.

Hunters and campers dislike the porcupine. In addition to the damage he does to dogs, porky will gnaw ax handles, canoe paddles, saddle rigging, and any other gear which has been soaked with sweat and contains salt.

Legal protection was once given this big rodent in many areas. As the animal can be killed with a heavy club, he was protected from hunters in order to serve as game

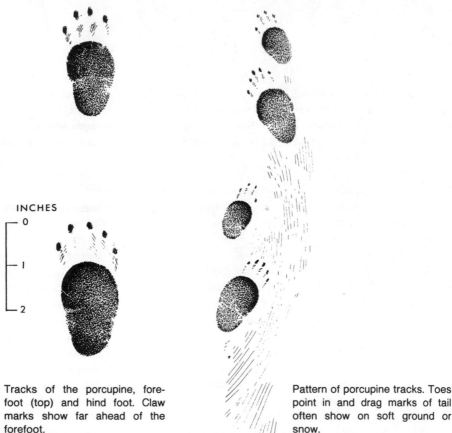

INCHES

0

1

2

Tracks of the porcupine, fore-foot (top) and hind foot. Claw marks show far ahead of the forefoot.

Pattern of porcupine tracks. Toes point in and drag marks of tail often show on soft ground or snow.

for anyone stranded in the wilds. However, the damage a porcupine does to timber and personal gear, to say nothing of the latent treachery of his armament, is now thought to outweigh this consideration and in many regions, especially timber areas, the porcupine is now considered a pest.

Porcupines can be killed with any kind of cartridge, largely because they can be approached very close without danger, and they make no fast attempts to get away. A .22 rimfire bullet will easily kill a porky. A head shot should always be taken as body shots simply wound this fat animal. A .38 Special handgun makes a fine weapon for the occasional porcupine found while tramping the woods and hills.

I used to wonder just how a lost person would skin and eat a porcupine, even if he had succeeded in killing it with a club. The Tahltan Indians of British Columbia told me that they handle them just like moose nose—a great delicacy. They toss the porky into a roaring fire which burns off all the quills. The burned hide can then be peeled off, exposing the flesh beneath.

Muskrat

21

Muskrat

THE MUSKRAT *(Ondatra zibethicus)* is a true fur-bearer and has long since surpassed the beaver in importance to the fur trade. This is partly because of the quality of his own fine fur, but also because muskrat fur can be processed to resemble more costly furs. This animal is usually trapped rather than hunted.

Many a rural youngster, with no more elaborate equipment than a half-dozen Victor #1 steel traps and a dozen red-cedar shingles, made his first spending money by trapping this small furry animal. The traps were set along the edge of a stream or slough where the magpie-like tracks and "slicked" mud showed the rats to be working. The hides of the trapped rats were stretched over the ogive-shaped ends of the shingles, and the dried hides shipped to some eastern fur buyer.

The muskrat, also called a marsh rabbit in some areas of the South where his flesh is eaten, is one of the most ubiquitous of our small animals. Forty-eight of our fifty states have muskrats, and the supply is kept up because the animal is so prolific. Depending somewhat upon latitude and food supply, the females have two or more litters per year for a total annual increase of fifteen to twenty young. The Delta country around the mouth of the Mississippi and Canada's lake areas are richly supplied with muskrats. As with other species, the best pelts often come from the northern latitudes, and such pelts are often darker in coloration.

Muskrats will grow to nearly 24 inches in length including the tail, which is about 10 inches long, scaly, flat, and without hair. The fur is a dark brown on the guard-hairs, which protrude from a thick layer of bluish-colored underfur. This underfur, incidentally, is the material from which the famed Gray Nymph trout fly is made.

The muskrat is a water-lover. He inhabits the banks of rivers, shores of lakes, and muddy swamp areas, feeding on aquatic plants and building his home a few feet from the water's edge. The home consists of a small shelf erected on the earth, with a rounded hut made of mud, sticks, and reeds constructed upon it. The house is reached via a tunnel dug at the surface of the water or just under it. The underwater inlet prevents land enemies such as foxes, weasels, and owls from getting at him. In areas where large lake fish live, the young rats are often gobbled up by such fish.

These inlet tunnels, however, are the best places to trap this animal, which is one of the easiest to trap. Setting a #1 steel trap in the mud at the bottom of the tunnel to a muskrat's house is nearly a sure-fire way of catching him.

This little fur-bearer doesn't fear man unduly and will often swim within a rod or so of people. Any sudden movement, however, will send him out of sight. Because of this lack of fear, muskrats are easy to shoot. In the North, many have been harvested for their hides with a .22 rimfire rifle. Just before sundown, hunters would

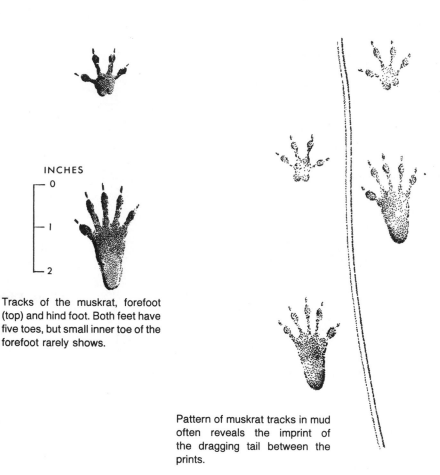

INCHES

0

1

2

Tracks of the muskrat, forefoot (top) and hind foot. Both feet have five toes, but small inner toe of the forefoot rarely shows.

Pattern of muskrat tracks in mud often reveals the imprint of the dragging tail between the prints.

Muskrat builds his house a few feet from the shoreline on a small shelf, forming a rounded hut of mud, sticks, and reeds. An underwater tunnel, leading from the shore to the hut, protects the animal from land enemies.

work the lake shores and slough edges, remaining as concealed as possible, and shoot the animals in the head as they came above water at the bank or as they climbed on the ice. Those shot while swimming near shore were often retrieved with a three-pronged snag hook and sinker of some kind tied to the end of a long fishing line—a miniature replica of the outfit used by Eskimos to retrieve hair seals.

Indians have told me of hair-raising experiences hunting muskrats in Alaska. As they have "worked" a region, shooting rats for their hides and skinning them out on the spot, grizzly bears have systematically followed them and eaten the carcasses. When the bear eventually caught up with the hunter, the Indian occasionally had to dispatch the bruin with his .22 rifle, a puny weapon to use against a grizzly.

It is questionable whether, in many areas, the muskrat will ever be reclassified from the status of fur-bearer to that of small game open to hunting. If he ever is, the technique of harvesting him will be simply to slowly walk the banks, shorelines, and cattail edges of water where visible spoor (tracks in the mud and bank entrances with slicked-down bottom earth) shows the animal to be; then head-shoot him as he appears out of the water with a .22 rimfire using long-rifle hollow-points. Early morning and late evening are the best times of day.

Skinning a muskrat is similar to skinning jack rabbit, with one exception. A sharp knife is used to girdle the ankles and to skin around the ears, eyes, and nose—whereas with jack rabbits, the skin may be twisted and broken, then pulled off. In each case, the hide is removed in the form of an unslitted sleeve. The hide is then stretched tightly over a shingle or board whose top has been tapered into a mild ogive shape. This taper will hold the front end of the hide stretched, and the tail end may then be fastened by nailing both sides of the hide to the board with shingle nails.

When you want to mount a muskrat or other small animal, the hide is not cased from the carcass. Instead, a slit is made from one foot to the opposing foot, for both front and hind feet, and a longitudinal cut is made from anus to throat. The entire carcass is removed through the opening created by these three incisions, by skinning back from them and then carefully removing all flesh and meat. The feet, tail, ears, and nose—including the entire septum—are left integral with the hide. This, plus heavy salting, will usualy keep a small hide until the taxidermist can be reached. He will place the hide around an artificial form and sew up all incisions so they don't show.

22

Opossum

THE OPOSSUM *(Didelphis virginiana),* or possum, as he is commonly called, is one of the few marsupials (pouched animals) found in North America which has survived from the Pleistocene period. As with other marsupials, such as the kangaroo in Australia, the pouch serves the useful purpose of protecting the young at the mother's body until they are large enough to move about.

This species is an odd, furry-looking creature somewhat resembling an oversized rat. The animal's nose is long and pointed, the tail and ears naked of hair, and the short-legged body lies close upon the ground or a limb.

An adult opossum achieves a length of about 30 inches and weighs up to 9 pounds. The tail is approximately 12 inches long and is prehensile—that is, it can be used for grasping. Both fore and hind feet have five toes, the first toe of the hind feet being spread for grasping, enabling the animal to swing from tree limbs by his hind feet as well as his tail. The opossum's fur is coarse and is usually gray above and whitish below. The face is white, and the ears and inner part of the tail are black.

The opossum is very prolific, with two broods in the South and one brood per year in the North being common. A brood consists of fifteen or more young, and the tiny infants are no bigger than peanuts. At birth, the young claw their way through the fur and into the female's pouch where they fasten onto a nipple and remain until they reach several times their original size. In two to three months the young are the size of field mice and emerge part of the time from the pouch. Danger will cause them to return to the pouch.

After reaching this size, the young opossums will begin to travel upon their

Opossum

INCHES

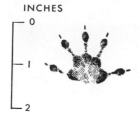

Pattern of opossum tracks. Front and hind feet may be side by side, or hind foot may be slightly behind forefoot as above.

Tracks of the opossum, forefoot (top) and hind foot. Toe of the hind foot slants inward or backward.

mother's back as she moves about and hunts for food—insects, tiny snakes and frogs, berries, fruits, and young corn.

The opossum generally inhabits woodlands in farming country, ranging from New York to Florida and from the Atlantic coast to the Great Lakes and Texas. Like the raccoon, the animal is migrating northward into southern Canada.

The presence of opossums is not detected in many areas simply because this species is purely nocturnal and normally comes out from hiding only at night. Opossums favor rocky dens, hollow trees, and logs, but often use the burrows of larger animals.

Opossums are generally hunted with dogs. The chase isn't nearly as exciting as a raccoon hunt, since the animal, on being flushed, usually heads for the nearest climbable tree and disappears into the branches. A .22 rifle using long-rifle hollow-points is suitable for shooting treed opossums. Open sights are preferable to telescopic sights, since opossums are shot at short range. Besides, a glass sight may be damaged during a night hunt.

Badger

23

Badger

I HAVE hunted many times with an old Montana outfitter who lived to his sixties without ever having married. He did not remain a bachelor by choice but because he devoted most of his life to caring for an invalid brother who had been thrown violently from a saddle horse and had injured his spine. The running horse had stepped into a badger hole.

Accidents such as this were common in the early days of the West and were the main reason why the badger was so thoroughly hated. This big, squat, burrowing animal *(Taxidea taxus)* would dig holes a foot or so across in the soft earth of arid and desert areas. Because of the foliage, these holes often could not be detected. A horse, or even a man, moving with any speed in range country, was as apt as not to step in a badger hole and come up minus the use of one leg. The animal also dug holes in agricultural lands which spoiled irrigation dikes and tipped over farm machinery.

In appearance the badger resembles the porcupine—and even more, the wolverine. All are bulky animals built low to the ground. The badger has a sharply pointed nose which recedes into a broad, flattish face having multiple stripes of gray-black and white. The body at the top has a thin, whitish stripe running its length and a short tail which is bushy and tipped with black. The claws are dark and long, with the curve and size necessary for heavy and continuous digging. Adult badgers will reach over 2 feet in their stubby length and weigh from 12 to 20 pounds. Among other members of the weasel family, only the wolverine is larger.

The original range of the badger was from the prairie lands of Canada in the Fort

St. John area to Mexico, and from the Mississippi Basin westward to the Pacific. Like many another species which has become extinct in certain regions, the badger now lives only in spot areas, principally in the Great Plains to the Rocky Mountains. His home is in arid lands, deserts, what sagebrush country still remains—areas of sparse human habitation.

As with other limited species, the badger is often shot by hunters who happen to be after other game. Jack rabbit hunters often spot a badger digging a new hole in the earth, and rockchuck hunters scanning the terrain with binoculars may see a badger moving about somewhere between his network of holes. The legality of hunting him in any area should be checked in advance.

If you want to hunt badgers exclusively, the first thing to do is to find evidence of their recent digging. Then post yourself about 100 yards from the area, concealed as much as possible in brush, or by camouflage clothing, and wait patiently. Early morning or late evening is a good time. Assuming the spoor is fresh, eventually the animal will emerge.

Any cartridge suitable for chucks will kill a badger—from the .22 WMR to the .222, .223, .224 Weatherby, .225, .22/250 . . . on up to the big-game rifle and cartridge you may be using.

INCHES

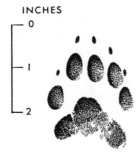

Badger tracks, forefoot (top) and hind foot.

Pattern of badger tracks. Prints are toed-in, long claws register clearly ahead of toe pads.

116

24

Beaver

PERHAPS NO animal in history has had as great an influence on the mass migration of a people as the beaver *(Castor canadensis)*. The explorers of the West and Canada returned with glowing reports of the animal's "inexhaustible" numbers, luring the fur companies and fur traders into the wilderness. These in turn told of the other bountiful resources of the new land, and the homesteaders and settlers came to lay the foundation for a lavish agrarian economy.

Like the "unlimited" bison and timber of the settled East, the "inexhaustible" supply of beavers was soon depleted. The beaver was subjected to the inevitable violent harvest, and in many areas he was threatened with actual extinction. Only with the enforcement of a system of game management, and the public realization that as a continent we were harvesting ourselves into collective poverty, did the beaver start his long comeback.

The beaver is our largest gnawing animal, or rodent. He is a chunky-looking animal with rich, brown fur and a short, flat tail which is scaled and oval-shaped. Both sexes look alike. Like the muskrat, the beaver has a woolly bluish undercoat necessary for spending long periods under water. The beaver's hind feet are webbed, leaving a track in the mud like that of a Canadian honker; the front ones are rather small and slender.

The beaver is a real engineer and a tireless worker. His principal activity is building dams across small creeks and streams. These dams are painstakingly made of interlaced sticks and sections of gnawed saplings. The tightness of the weave, plus the accumulation of leaves and moss against the face side as the current moves them

Beaver

INCHES

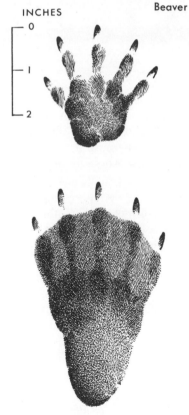

Beaver tracks, forefoot (top) and hind foot. Large, webbed hind-foot print is identifying sign.

Pattern of beaver tracks. Fore and hind feet appear close together. Often all five toes of forefoot do not register.

into position, make a beaver dam nearly waterproof. The topmost edge of the dam is always perfectly horizontal, regardless of the water stage during construction.

The dam is built to create a pond whose purpose is twofold. First, it provides a place for the beaver to build his house. This house must be safe from flooding, and this calls for a constant water level. Any fluctuation due to spring runoff or cloud bursts is regulated by the long unobstructed top of the dam, which will spread out this excess water and not raise the level appreciably. In the pond, upon an elevated platform, the beaver builds a dome-shaped structure of sticks, saplings, reeds, bark, and mud, often larger than the average room of a house. The entrance is under water.

The second function of the pond is to provide a storage place for tree branches which the beaver floats down the enlarged creek. The principal food of the beaver is the bark of alders and quaking aspens, or popple of the North. Branches of these, as well as of other species, are moved into the pond and adjacent to the house. The bark is used for food and the stalks for more building. In fairly level areas, beavers have been known to dig channels for several hundred yards, in which to move small logs. In Wyoming, I have seen places where a beaver had pulled sections of aspen twice his 50-pound size into Elk Creek, and had floated them down a quarter-mile to his house and pond. Within this region there are aspens 2 feet in diameter which have been felled by gnawing beavers.

The beaver is monogamous. Mating occurs in January and February, with a litter of two to possibly eight kits being born in April or May. As in the case of mountain goats, the young beavers are driven from the home upon the arrival of new young. With beavers this occurs in the second year. On leaving the old home, the two-year-olds will pair off, mate, and generally build a home of their own in the same general region. As a local beaver colony grows, the tendency is to work downstream.

Now, after his long comeback, the beaver is harvested only as a fur animal. In many regions the state or province will manage the harvest, either trapping the animals which represent an excess to a particular area, or leasing out the trapping privileges to an individual on a limited-permit basis. This is often done in agricultural country where a beaver population has multiplied, moved downstream into a network of canals and irrigation systems, and has begun to do real damage. Often the rancher on whose land this damage occurs will be granted the privilege of trapping a given number.

On the other hand, beavers are often flown into watershed country to start new dams for the express purpose of reinstating springs and small creeks which dry up otherwise and ruin valuable range country. The animals, in pairs, are parachuted down in crates which will open upon impact, and the animals take it from there. In many instances, after the introduction of beavers into an area, creeks which otherwise would dry up run all season and the springs feeding from them are rehabilitated.

The current range of the beaver generally coincides with his original distribution —over most of North America from Alaska to Texas, in the stream and lake areas. Due to his depleted numbers, however, he now lives in localized areas.

Beavers have little fear of man and are occasionally made into pets. When swimming along the bank of a lake or river, they will often allow man to come within 30

The beaver is a tireless worker and an expert engineer. He builds a dam of sticks, leaves, and mud (above) to keep the water level of the stream constant and prevent flooding his carefully constructed lodge (below).

yards or so. Then, after ascertaining his intent, they will dive, slapping their broad tails with a loud report. Often these slappings will be heard all night near a beaver colony, advertising the boundless energy of the species.

Although the beaver is purely a fur species and is harvested by trapping, he belongs with the group of small American game animals. He is part of the wildlife scene. Observing him and his ingenious and intricate handiwork is a vital part of enjoying the outdoors.

INDEX

Index